THE GARDEN

by Philip Swindells

Illustrated by Petra Stanton

"ERROR FREE PRODUCT WITH EXCEPTIONAL SERVICE"

TOTAL QUALITY

Contents

Site and soil

Whether you are looking at your existing garden with a view to getting the best from it, or are faced with someone else's creation, time spent making a proper assessment of the site and understanding the soil, is very well spent. Decisions that are made in the beginning greatly influence the success of the venture.

Aspect

The aspect of the garden is very important – both exposure and elevation. Each have a marked effect upon the ability of the gardener to grow satisfactory plants. Nothing much can be done about the effects of elevation, but shelter can be provided to reduce some of the problems of exposure.

The careful placing of fences, walls or hedges can create microclimates of surprising softness on the harshest and most exposed of sites. When putting together a plan for the garden give very serious consideration to these factors. Indeed, many gardeners assert that wind is their greatest enemy. The choice of windbreaks is discussed on page 24.

The soil

The greatest influence exerted upon a garden is the soil. It not only has a profound effect upon the growth of plants, but also the features which can be successfully created and maintained within a garden. Soil, according to the dictionary, is 'the uppermost layer of the earth in which plants grow and which has been formed from disintegrating rocks and accumulated organic matter'.

This rather dry statement in its broadest sense is correct, however, it should be appreciated that the rocks which through the ages have formed the soil in one district are quite likely to be vastly different from those that have formed the soil a few miles away. It is therefore essential to appreciate right from the outset that soil is a widely variable substance with different properties that need different treatments to achieve similar results.

There are basically two types of soil; light and heavy. Light soil is light in weight, not in colour as is often supposed, and generally of a rather coarse texture with large particles. These are chiefly of sand and give rise to large air spaces which assist with the free passage of water.

Heavy soils on the other hand are composed of very fine particles which pack closely together, retaining moisture readily and quickly become caked and sticky, or when dried out setting in a concrete-like mass. Few soils are at the extremes of heaviness or lightness, but it is also true to say that few would not be improved by careful cultivation and the sensible use of organic matter.

Light soils need the addition of moisture retaining materials such as cow or pig manure or old leaves or compost. The regular hoeing of crops during the summer months also assists with retaining moisture, while surface mulches of old leaves or well rotted lawn mowings around individual plants and bushes are most beneficial.

Heavy soils conversely require lightening and opening up and this can be achieved by digging in quantities of straw, strawy manure, sand, grit, clinker or indeed any other materials of a coarse texture. Clay soils with a relatively low alkalinity can be much improved by the addition of lime sprinkled evenly over the surface and then lightly raked in. This causes flocculation of the clay particles – the collecting and separating of colonies of tiny particles which under the physical influence of the lime form larger particles which in turn make the soil lighter.

Soils of many varying textures and constituents exist, such as peaty, alluvial, marl, loam, but all can be classified with some degree of accuracy under the heading of light or heavy.

Apart from the very obvious visible characteristics there are those unseen which are of equal importance to the grower, but infinitely more difficult to ascertain. The degree of acidity and alkalinity is one of these, although modern science has brought a simple kit to the garden shop which is readily available and easily used giving a surprising measure of accuracy. The theory and reasoning behind the method of measuring acidity and alkalinity is complex and does not bear relating here. It is sufficient to say that a pH of 7.0 indicates a neutral soil, one higher, say of 8.0, alkaline, and those of lower numerals acid.

Gardeners on acid soils are the more fortunate as it is easy to correct excessive acidity or create alkalinity by the addition of hydrated lime, but on an alkaline soil it is very difficult to reverse the process. All one can hope to do is adjust to neutrality by incorporating plenty of organic matter during cultivation or adding limited quantities of aluminium sulphate.

Most plants will grow on a soil containing lime as calcium is of considerable nutrient value to them and the influence of alkalinity increases the activity of soil borne organisms in creating and breaking down humus. Unfortunately, the presence of lime also inhibits the absorbtion of phosphorus and iron, and in certain plants such as heathers and rhododendrons this induces chlorosis or yellowing of the leaves.

Persistent gardeners on an alkaline soil can alleviate this condition by the use of an iron chelate compound watered around susceptible plants during the growing season, but subsequent growth is not comparable with that of plants growing under natural acidic conditions.

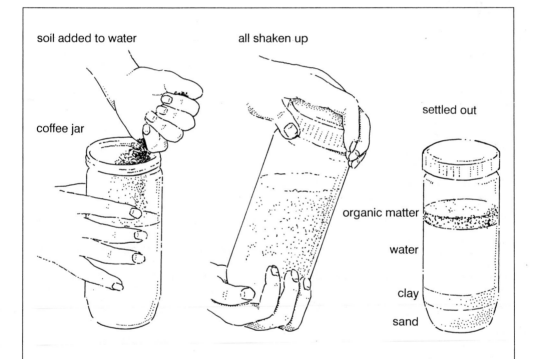

soil added to water

all shaken up

coffee jar

settled out

organic matter

water

clay

sand

Down-to-earth tip

If you wish to determine accurately the amounts of clay and sand particles in your soil, then make a simple test. Take two or three tablespoons of dry soil, rub it down into a powder and place in a coffee jar. Add water and shake vigorously until it is just muddy water. Stand and allow to settle. The larger sand particles will settle within an hour. The clay may take two or three days. Any organic matter will float on the surface of the water. After four or five days the water will have completely cleared and a layer each of sand and clay will have been deposited on the bottom of the jar. Once your soil structure is known appropriate treatments can be applied.

Surveying the garden

It is very important to survey your garden before putting together a plan. This is not the kind of survey that a professional surveyor might make, but a sensible appraisal of the site.

The first task

The first task is to make a study of existing trees, hedges and buildings, indeed anything that is likely to affect plant growth. Consideration should also be given to the position of any building, such as a shed or greenhouse, which you may build during the next couple of years. Tall hedges and overhanging trees should be noted as requiring pruning in order to allow access for sunlight and the free passage of air.

Buildings are, of course, a permanent feature, but ways in which they can be used if forming a boundary, or any benefits that can be derived through sheltering plants from the wind or shading those that desire it, should be considered during the survey.

The survey

Before a definite plan can be drawn up there are a number of facts that must be determined. As indicated earlier, a knowledge of soil conditions is vital. To ascertain these take a soil profile. This is broadly speaking a hole which is dug sufficiently deep enough to expose to view the varying layers of material that form the top couple of feet of soil as this has a considerable bearing upon operations such as drainage which may be necessary before cultivation can begin.

The approximate relationships of different soil levels to one another and the house are also important. By taking a good stout plank of wood devoid of twists and unevenness, a handful of strong wooden stakes and a spirit level a reasonably accurate picture can be obtained. The board is used on edge with the spirit level lying along the upper edge. Stakes are then progressively knocked into the ground at slightly less distance than the board's length.

A definite fixed level such as the back doorstep is taken as a starting point and a stake knocked into the ground so that the board and spirit level can be rested on both step and stake, the latter being knocked slowly into the ground until the board and spirit level show a level reading. The end of the board that rested on the step is placed on the stake and another stake pushed into the ground at a suitable distance and in the same manner.

From each of these stakes fresh ones can be put in level so that the overall effect is diamond or triangular patterns of level stakes which, if connected by strings attached to small tacks on their tops, will reveal the true lie of the land beneath.

Of course this method is not 100% accurate and to do the job properly back checking with the board from certain 'master' stakes to the others will ensure the minimum of error is transmitted from one to the other. However, it is a good general guide as to how the ground rises and falls, which is difficult to ascertain with the naked eye.

In order to ascertain the various positions of trees and other permanent garden features it is necessary to establish a base line. Knock two stakes in the ground 3 ft from the house wall and parallel to it. Attach a string. Measure fixed points along the base line so that two measurements can be taken to the object to be plotted. If a triangle with sides of fixed length can be achieved, with the object at its apex, its position can be readily transferred to paper.

The boundary

Established gardens have hedges and fences of varying types and it is undesirable to tamper with these unless they restrict light or the free flow of air. Great care is necessary in altering such barriers when they form a common boundary with a neighbour and his co-operation should be sought from the outset. Take advantage in a new garden without such barriers to use suitable materials to form a boundary of overall benefit to the garden.

Down-to-earth tip

When surveying a new garden and you are unsure of the acidity or alkalinity of the soil, look at the weed cover. The presence of sorrel or foxgloves guarantees an acid soil. Chickweed and groundsel indicate neutral or alkaline conditions. Vetches and old man's beard usually indicate chalky soil.

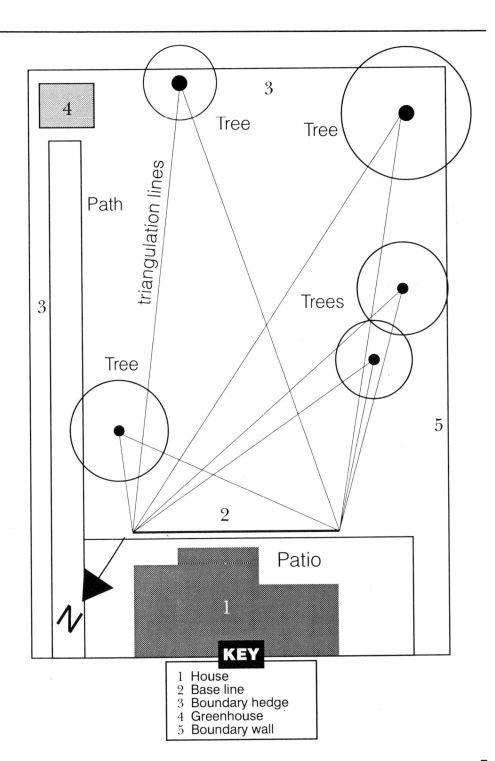

KEY
1 House
2 Base line
3 Boundary hedge
4 Greenhouse
5 Boundary wall

Garden layout

Having made a simple survey of the site it is useful to commit it to paper and juggle your ideas around with pencil and ruler. Rarely will any gardener produce a plan on paper that he will stick to, but the production of an outline strategy for the garden with guidelines for the future is invaluable.

The plan

Graph paper is useful for making a plan, for then each square can represent a fixed measurement. Existing features should be marked and for a realistic appraisal of the situation a few scale cut-outs in card of large trees, buildings or any other features of the immediate landscape should be made and erected on the plan. This gives an idea of the effect each feature will have on the garden.

The placing of any buildings should be decided and the position of paths drawn in. Paths should not be skimped, for although they occupy valuable ground they are the lifeline of the garden if neglect of areas through difficulty of access is to be avoided. One good wide path sufficient to take a wheelbarrow with ease, and also the garden cultivator should you have one, is preferable to numerous narrower paths where the wheelbarrow handles catch in the vegetation or the rotavator blades scythe down treasured plants. If a cultivator is to be used in the garden then beds or borders should be made compatible with axle or tool bar widths. If a machine might be bought, hired or borrowed from a neighbour later, but the actual width is unknown, then allow a minimum border width of 4 ft.

The placing of trees and shrubs must be carefully considered for once established they resent disturbance. Recommended distances should be adhered to. Half standard apple trees may look better planted 5 ft. apart when received from the nursery, but within four or five years will become a terrible mess incapable of proper care and cultivation unless thinned to the recommended distance. Close planting of woody plants to paths should similarly be avoided.

Consider the proximity of plants to the house. Plants such as thyme and mint that are frequently used should be placed as close to the kitchen door as feasible, while the vegetable plot should be a trifle more distant and the fruit garden should occupy the outlying parts of the garden. Every square foot of soil capable of supporting plant life should be carefully considered. An odd patch by the garden shed may support a loganberry, the narrow border alongside the house a grape vine. Where space is limited or no open ground is available, such as in a small courtyard or even on a balcony, plan the sensible use of pots, boxes and tubs for subjects to which they are suited.

Levels and drainage

Having decided the position of each permanent feature and having marked them carefully on the plan, consider the various levels of the plot and the method of drainage to be employed if necessary.

Steeply sloping ground may be difficult to work and heavy rain may lead to erosion of the top soil. This can be remedied by terracing, using one or maybe two retaining walls and then levelling the soil into two or three plateaus. Uneven ground, if marked out with stakes of even height, is relatively simple to level to gentle slopes which are easy on the eye, back and machine. However, it is imperative to be clear on the plan as to which way the land falls, or is likely to fall after necessary correction, before a scheme for drainage is devised.

This need not be a complicated affair, for the average garden is not vast, and no more than two or three tracks will be required to ensure adequate drainage. It is illegal to connect land drainage to the public sewer or even the thick gravel bed which these drains rest on. In most cases it would be impractical to do so even if this were possible and so it is wise to consult one's own deeds or local documents to try to discover where common drains run.

Perhaps there is a brook or parish ditch close by into which surface water may flow. When a discovery of this type is successfully made, then the disposal of water seldom presents any problems. It is only when one has drawn a blank that any problems arise. If the worst comes to the worst the use of one or possibly two soakaways will do much to alleviate waterlogging if not entirely overcoming the drainage problem.

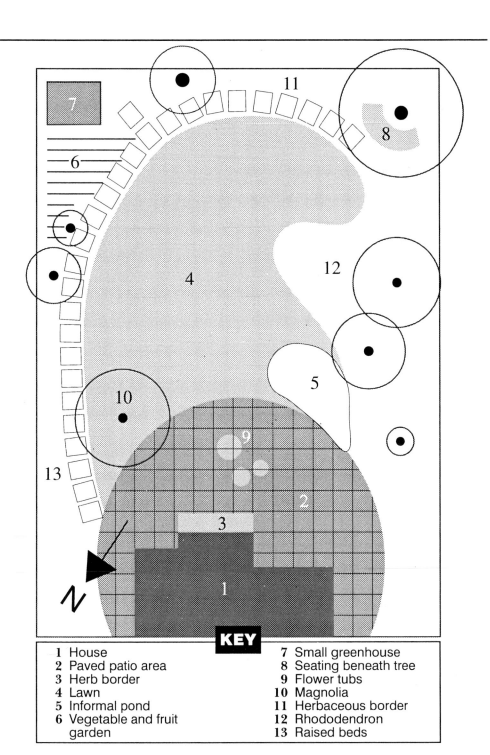

KEY

1 House
2 Paved patio area
3 Herb border
4 Lawn
5 Informal pond
6 Vegetable and fruit
  garden
7 Small greenhouse
8 Seating beneath tree
9 Flower tubs
10 Magnolia
11 Herbaceous border
12 Rhododendron
13 Raised beds

Tools and machinery

For a gardener to be successful he must have the right tools and machinery. Hand tools in particular should be of a quality and manufacture which ensure that the work can be done properly. Indeed, professional gardeners regard tools as extensions of their hands.

Hand tools

For the majority of home gardeners hand tools are all that is required, except perhaps for a lawn mower. The first priority is a spade. For women the kind popularly referred to as the border spade is ideal as it is not too heavy. This is reasonably narrow and lightweight, its original function being for work amongst plants and shrubs in a border.

Most men will be able to handle a digging spade without difficulty. This is heavy, solid and with a wide blade and is intended for turning over soil for the winter.

The same can be achieved with a border spade, but being of smaller dimensions the digging takes very much longer. All spades come with either D or T shaped handles, so before selecting your tool it is advisable to have a practice dig to see which handle shape suits you best. It is also vital to be comfortable with the weight and balance of the tool.

The same applies to garden forks. The order fork is an exceptionally useful tool for forking through existing borders and is ideal for lady gardeners. Digging forks come in two main kinds, those with round tines used for general cultivation and the ones with flat tines that are intended for digging potatoes and making excavations in heavy soil.

There are a number of different styles of hoe. Although mostly used for hoeing out weeds and keeping the ground tidy, the swan neck hoe is also used for making seed drills. It is used either on edge to create a V shaped drill or flat to make a flat-bottomed drill.

The Dutch or push hoe is for cutting off weeds at ground level with a pushing motion while the more recently introduced

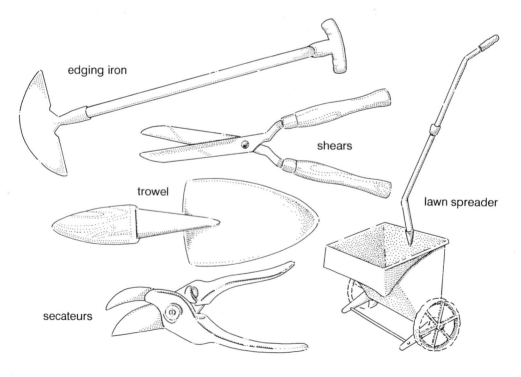

edging iron

shears

trowel

lawn spreader

secateurs

swoe destroys weeds with a pull and push action.

Rakes come in all shapes and sizes, but the common garden rake is the most versatile. This is mostly used for levelling cultivated soil and tidying up seed beds but it can be utilised for most raking requirements. Leaves and cut grass are best gathered together with a spring tine rake, although some gardeners favour those with wooden tines.

Trowels are fairly standard but it is false economy to buy a cheap tool. Unless they are of high quality the handle will regularly snap at the point where it joins the blade.

It is surprising how much pressure is applied to a trowel during ordinary domestic garden use. In addition to the common trowel there are narrow bladed kinds for working in confined spaces and bulb planting trowels which have graduations along their length to ensure a uniform depth of planting.

Hand forks are used for careful weeding amongst established plants and are especially valuable for working in pockets on the rock garden. So are the small hand cultivators that look rather like enlarged back scratchers. These come in larger sizes too and are often the mainstay of the weed control programme on the vegetable plot.

Shears are perhaps not as fashionable now as hedge trimmers when it comes to cutting hedges. Indeed, the modern rechargeable, go-anywhere electrical trimmer has revolutionised hedge cutting.

However, shears will still be found to be invaluable, particularly during the autumn for cutting back fading herbaceous plants. They can also be used regularly on heathers and the various cushion-forming rock garden plants as soon as they have finished flowering.

Secateurs tend to be used for faded shrubs, flowers and also, of course, for pruning. The variety of secateurs available is confusing. There is no particular kind that is any better than another. It is a matter of personal choice and what feels the most comfortable. Quality is important though, for secateurs, like trowels, take a lot of wear and a poor quality product will soon fall to pieces.

Lawn edging shears come into a similar category. These should be of top quality and yet lightweight. They are used to ensure that the edge of the lawn is neat and razor sharp. Before they can regularly achieve this the turf edge has to be straight and in good order. This is done with an edging iron or half moon.

Although perhaps used once a year for this purpose it is a very useful tool to have in the potting shed. It can be used very well for cutting out new beds and features and is invaluable if you have to lift and move any turf.

The lawn mower

Lawn mowers are very confusing to the beginner. There are several different kinds and within these numerous brands with varying cutting widths. For a pristine lawn that consists of fine grasses a cylinder mower is best. The majority have eight blades on the cylinder, but it is possible to buy models with up to sixteen blades. The more blades the mower has the finer the cut. A grass collecting box is also an essential addition for a machine that is to be used on a fine sward.

Rotary mowers are good for hard-wearing lawns and rough grass. Most have a significant raise and lower adjustment which means that a neat lawn can be maintained, but at the same time there is a facility to cut longer grass such as that in which bulbs have been naturalised. For sloping areas a hover mower is to be preferred. This will go into most places, but with few exceptions is unable to produce the attractive lawn stripes that most gardeners prefer.

The wheelbarrow

Finally we have the wheelbarrow. A builder's barrow is far better than any garden barrow, unless you are not strong enough to wheel it when loaded. Modern garden wheelbarrows are fine for pushing a few weeds around in, but the builder's barrow is what is necessary for moving soil, rocks or paving. If you are going to have a standard garden wheelbarrow, then choose one of the models with two wheels. These are more stable and resilient than the traditional one wheeled kind.

11

Plot skills

The gardener has to develop many skills in order to produce a successful flower garden or vegetable harvest. While experience and the passage of time hone these, it is necessary to understand the basics to begin with. Bad habits are difficult to break, however, traditional methods are not always all they may appear to be and so a happy medium must be adopted.

Digging

The proposals put forward here are unlikely to be found in many respected text books, but experience shows that they are the best. Ignore all the plethora of names appended to different forms of the digging operation - double digging, single digging, bastard trenching and so on. Also ignore the often complicated diagrams showing plot A and plot B and how the soil from the trench in plot A should be wheeled to the far end of plot B for replacement at the end of digging operations. Gardeners are practical people, and while erring on the side of caution when anything new is revealed, usually pick out the best aspects of traditional and new methods and come to a compromise. For most gardeners this is the case with digging, those who propose the more complex methods rarely being the ones who undertake them.

Few gardeners practice double digging now. Most realise the folly of digging down two spades deep and breaking up the soil, except for certain exceptional circumstances. However, the value of single digging when sensibly applied is widely appreciated. Single digging is the turning over or completely inverting lumps of soil so that the surface which is covered with plant growth is completely buried. This is only performed on cultivated land, not rough unbroken soil.

For rough land trenching is the best method of knocking the soil into shape. It is not only used for trench conditions but can be utilised within the well cultivated bed or border too. Trenching is the inverting of the soil in the first row as with single digging. Un-

1 Trenching

For trenching, dig at right angles to slice a spadeful of soil.

2 Filling in

Incorporate manure if desired then fill in with excavated soil.

conventionally, but sensibly, the second row is inverted on the top of the first. An open trench is then revealed which will accept each row of digging as the soil is turned over – and turned over is the operative word, for weeds will not die if the spadeful is merely tipped on one side, reversal must be complete.

This slightly unconventional method of starting trenching leads to a raised first row and a trench at the end of the bed, but this is of no account as the trench facilitates drainage during the winter when the soil is upturned and is easily filled when the soil is knocked down and raked level. This slight inconvenience is nothing compared with the interminable barrowing of soil which the writers of purist texts would have us perform. A bare bed or border waiting to be dug can be a formidable and disheartening spectacle. Psychologically it is better to take narrow strips a yard or so wide and dig these the full length of the bed in succession. Obviously, the ground is not covered any faster, but the illusion is that this is so.

Hoeing

The use of the hoe is vital for weed control, especially on the vegetable or fruit plot. It can also be used for creating drills for seed sowing. The most useful hoe is the swan neck type. This is multi-purpose being useful for weeds, but essential for making seed drills. The hoeing action in the removal of weeds is a steady backwards and forwards movement with the blade held flush to the ground. The gardener walks forwards, the hoe being used in a smooth chopping motion before him. Unlike the flat Dutch or push hoe, the swan neck type is easily manoeuvred to remove weeds effortlessly from amongst plants and shrubs.

To take out a drill with a hoe it is necessary to first put down a garden line. This can be as simple as a length of string attached to two short canes which mark out where you intend to sow the seeds. Make sure that it is tight and then with the hoe blade on edge and resting against the taut string a V shaped drill is drawn out. The line is removed and the seeds sown in the drill and then gently covered with soil dragged over by the hoe. Some vegetable seeds like peas

and beans go into flat bottomed drills. These require a line putting in place but then the hoe is used flat to create what amounts to a very shallow trench, no more than an inch deep, the width of the hoe blade. The seeds are spaced out in the drill and soil is gently dragged back over.

The Dutch hoe or push hoe has a flat blade that more or less lies horizontal to the soil. The gardener pushes it towards the weeds, cutting them off at ground level. The action is of push and withdraw. It is a very effective and a swift way of dealing with young weeds, especially amongst rows of vegetables. Some gardeners like to create a dust mulch which amounts to a shallow layer of finely cultivated soil which is regularly moved, but which then serves as a moisture conserving layer. Advocates of this acceptable method of cultivation always recommend a push hoe for creating the kind of mulch desired.

Raking

The rake is a most useful tool, for not only is it vital for seed bed preparation, but it can also be used for scarifying, gathering debris and putting a fine finish on a cultivated bed or border.

The garden rake has teeth rather like nails and is the most versatile of tools. It is used in a pull and push motion to disturb and level the soil prior to sowing, whether it be a vegetable patch, flower border or lawn. Raking usually follows the passage of winter on an upturned soil, the weathered crumbly tilth being levelled out. To ensure a good firm seed bed, raking should be accompanied to begin with by shuffling.

This shuffling process is done with the feet, working sideways across the area to be raked. This firms the ground and ensures a good seed bed as well as making the raking process very much easier.

Unlike the hoe, the rake is used in a backwards pulling motion, the gardener drawing debris towards him. The raked seed bed surface, unlike the hoed surface, is not walked upon after the operation is complete. To ensure a good firm surface, raking should be accompanied by shuffling and slight compaction of the soil with the feet.

Pruning: Fruit

Much of what is written here also applies to decorative trees and shrubs. The various simple pruning methods that are applicable to canes and soft bushes are to be found with their general cultural requirements.

Choosing the right tools

There is a wide range of tools that can be used for pruning, many favoured for different purposes. The most frequently used are the secateurs. These are available in a wide range of shapes and sizes with special pairs being made for left handed gardeners. Being very strong cutters, they can take flimsy stems through to wood about half an inch in in diameter. Some can even tackle thicker material without straining.

Most gardeners do not realise that there is a correct method of holding secateurs when pruning. They should be placed in the hand the right way up. That is the slim blade facing the material to be retained and the anvil adjacent that to be disposed of. The thicker blade, or anvil, tends to crush stems, so must always face away from the bush.

Parrot bills are more substantial pruners of a similar pattern to secateurs, but take much thicker material. These are different designs, some with flat, straight edged blades like those of most secateurs. Others, the true parrot bills, in which the blades are curved and very reminiscent of the beak of a parrot.

In their more advanced state, but usually of a slightly different design, they appear as loppers on an extended pole. A handle at the lower end depends upon a leverage mechanism to enable the blades to snap shut on a branch in the tree canopy while the operator stands on the ground.

General pruning

Pruning is one of the most important, yet misunderstood gardening operations. There are many reasons for pruning. The most obvious one is to contain the growth of the

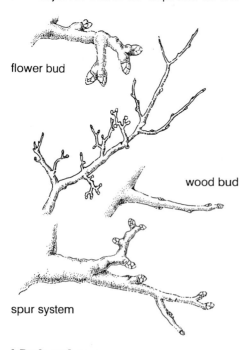

flower bud

wood bud

spur system

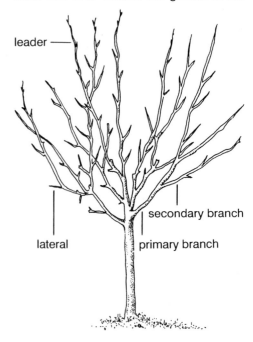

leader

secondary branch

lateral   primary branch

1 Buds and spurs

Flower bud, spur, spur system and wood buds on an apple tree branch.

2 Branches

Open centre bush apple tree with primary and secondary brances, leader and lateral.

tree and develop a shape which is not only visually appealing but practical to work with. This is often related to a specific kind of training which produces a tree of a shape and size compatible with the area or space available. Such pruning has to be conducted with the knowledge of the behaviour of the rootstock upon which the desirable tree is grafted. Regular pruning is necessary to maintain trained trees in good order.

Pruning also affects crop production. The reduction of weak, badly placed or excessive growth can lead to much improved quality and a heavier yield. Not only is this desirable in itself, but trees that are carefully manicured generally grow more lustily and have a greater resistance to pests and diseases. Not that this should be considered a prime reason for pruning, for the effect is slight. However, it remains a fact that in a well branched fruit tree with a good open framework air circulation is much improved and the likelihood of fungal diseases getting a hold is reduced.

On occasions when pests and diseases have ravaged plant tissue, it is often necessary to prune to remove damaged shoots and branches. A sort of vegetative surgery.

Formative pruning is vital for all fruit trees. If you purchase a poor quality herbaceous plant it is relatively simple to nurture, feed and turn it into a strong vigorous one. A fruit tree is a different proposition as it can quickly become set in a mis-shapen pattern. Only formative pruning can correct it and then only if caught in time. Not that it is desirable to purchase a mis-shapen tree.

The basic idea behind pruning apples and pears is to build a good strong framework in a young tree and control growth so that the maximum number of fruiting spurs are produced evenly along suitable branches. With stone fruits it is the encouragement of strong lateral shoots.

The removal of suckers – adventitious growths which arise from the rootstock – is also important as they compete with the desirable part of the tree for light and nourishment. Cuts on any parts of the tree should be made cleanly with a good pair of secateurs and in a slanting fashion in order to allow moisture to run off. They are generally made close to an outward pointing bud, but

not so close as to damage the bud nor so distant that a length of stem is left that will die back and allow the entry of fungal spores.

Young growths are generally cut back by about one third during the tree's formative life to encourage a stout framework. Weak or crossing branches and those likely to rub against one another are also removed, as well as any excess of fruiting spurs when dealing with established trees. Excess is determined as a congestion of growth which produces fruits, but leads to a decline in quality, mainly because the fruits are too close to one another and cannot develop properly. Fruits should not touch and there should be sufficient air circulation to discourage establishment of fungal diseases.

Remedial pruning

Pruning is not only a technique to develop and maintain fruit trees in good order, it is also a method of restoring overgrown specimens. If they are to slip into old age gracefully, whether they have been neglected or not, mature fruit trees require careful, regular attention. The often prolific growth of adventitious shoots from the trunk and around the base of established trees for example, not only looks unsightly, but diverts the flow of plant foods from their main course into superfluous growth. Annual removal, before the tissue hardens and becomes woody, controls the problem and prevents the appearance of unsightly scars and the formation of corky protruberances on the bark. When a tree has been neglected and these shoots are hard and woody they should be cut flush with the trunk.

Crowded or misplaced branches must all be removed. Limbs which cross and rub against one another can produce lesions which are then open to infection. Removing a sizeable branch requires a certain amount of expertise. The greatest problem is the weight of the limb. If it is just allowed to fall after cutting it will strip the bark from the remainder of the branch and often down the trunk as well. To prevent this occurring the limb should be under-cut sufficiently to sever the bark. Large branches can often be roped to those above in order to take the strain during the cutting process.

15

Pruning: Decorative plants

For most decorative plants the objectives of pruning are based upon a desire for the good production of flower, foliage and fruit, while at the same time keeping the tree or shrub shapely. This we might refer to as maintenance pruning.

Maintenance pruning

While most maintenance pruning is of large established frameworks, in the case of some trees, such as *Paulownia*, there is a renewal system which demands regular attention. However, the principles behind dealing with an established branched tree structure are in many respects not too dissimilar to those from a tree demanding a renewal regime.

Coloured stemmed trees and shrubs are normally subjected to a system known as stooling. This is the annual pruning back of all the previous season's growth in the spring after the stems have been enjoyed during the winter. Await the bursting of fresh young buds and then reduce the stems back to within two buds of the base.

Undertaken at bud break this ensures maximum length of stem production the following season. Only these stems of vigorous growth provide colour. Older wood always becomes dull and uninteresting.

Maintenance pruning is undertaken mainly to ensure the production of good, strong, productive branches in an arrangement which permits both the free circulation of air and easy care. By always pruning to an outward pointing bud there is every expectation of an outward growing branch developing. This can be adjusted as it grows if necessary by pruning later to a more upright pointing axillary bud if the branch is not growing in the manner desired. As leafy growth always reaches to the light, outward pointing buds usually yield upward to slightly outward pointing branches without the necessity for correction.

Developing a shape

The various training techniques pertinent to each kind of tree or shrub are nearly as numerous as the plants upon which the techniques are practised. To outline these it is useful to consider the development of a standard tree or shrub. One which has a clear stem and then a branched head. Whether grown on its own roots, or bottom worked – that is grafted close to the ground – the initial aim is to produce a straight clean stem as quickly as possible.

The aim of the first couple of year's growth is to produce the stem without any check in growth. Staking is very important from the outset. A good straight stem owes as much to the stake supporting it as to the speed of growth achieved. There is no need in the early stages to use a full size tree stake. A strong bamboo cane is perfectly adequate. It is important that a support is inserted from the outset and as the plant grows it is tied in and the side shoots are removed. Do not remove leaves at this stage as they are aiding growth and development.

Towards the end of the first season the lower leaves can be removed. They can be taken off sooner if it is thought that unsightly calluses and indentations might result. This is particularly pertinent to smaller standards like those of fuchsia or heliotrope where the entire stem is much more slender and likely to be made in a season. The removal of foliage, like most other pruning matters, is a question of personal judgement irrespective of the plant under consideration. Once the desired stem height is achieved the head can start forming.

Down-to-earth tip

If you are not sure how to prune your tree or shrub in order to get the best from it, then look at where it flowers and fruits. If it is grown for its foliage or stem colour, then observe the age of the wood that produces it – usually that of the past season.

When flowers and fruits are produced on the current season's growth, then cut it back early each spring. When on the past season's growth then cut out as much old wood as possible.

When produced on old wood, shorten back all new growths to a couple of buds. Even without knowing what the tree or shrub is you will have reasonable success.

The production of three or four good strong laterals are encouraged which are then carefully pinched or cut back to make a shapely head with an open framework. With some garden trees where large foliage is desired the laterals are reduced annually to a few buds but with trees where a more substantial structure is the aim they are pruned in a manner which not only keeps the tree to the desired shape but encourages the proliferation of flowering spurs.

Restoration pruning

Pruning is not only a technique to develop and maintain trees and shrubs in good order, it is a method of restoring overgrown or aged specimens. With some trees, such as willows, it is a case of cutting them hard back when they are of a variety that is likely to re-shoot evenly or removing them entirely if cutting back severely is unlikely to be successful. The majority of trees are a different proposition. They are so majestic and take so long to grow that the tendency is quite naturally to try to rejuvenate them and extend their useful life.

With a neglected tree, all branches that show signs of decay should be removed, together with any which outwardly appear to be healthy but which display the fruiting bodies of fungi. These are most frequently seen during the autumn and are an indication that all is not well. Soft areas sometimes appear on the trunk. These can be associated with mechanical damage or the attentions of browsing animals which delight in stripping the protective bark.

A tree that is in good health will quickly regenerate its covering of bark provided that this has not been removed from the entire circumference of the trunk. However, if the tissue beneath has also been damaged then decay may set in. If this is not too severe the soft pulpy tissue can be chiselled out and filled with concrete or fibreglass. It is even possible with large gaping holes to fill with concrete and retain this with brickwork. With the passing of time the tree will completely enclose the repair.

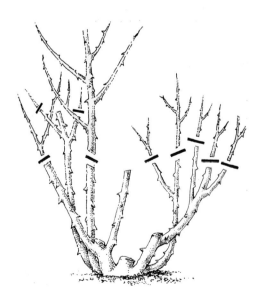

1 Root pruning

Cut back thicker roots with a pruning saw to check excess vigour.

2 Stem pruning

Cut back strong stems to 9 ins. and less vigorous stems and laterals to 6ins.

Propagation: Seed raising

Many plants can be raised from seed cheaply and efficiently. The principles of raising half-hardy bedding plants from seeds are discussed under that heading. Here we are considering raising plants from seed sown directly in the open ground and the specialised needs of certain plants which find germination difficult under either of these conditions.

Sowing directly outdoors

Some seeds, particularly those of hardy annual flowers, must be sown directly outside in the open ground. However, success with these plants owes as much to autumn and winter cultivations as those which are undertaken during the spring.

A deeply dug soil which has had plenty of organic matter incorporated into it and has then been left to the mercy of the elements for the winter months is ideal. This will retain moisture during dry periods and if

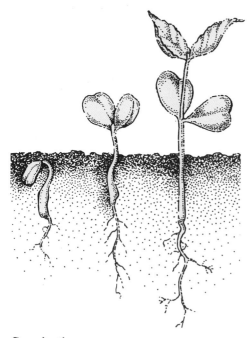

Germination

The stages of germination in seeds sown directly into open ground

well weathered will knock down with a hoe into a good friable soil that will provide conditions for seed sowing.

Spring dug soil, or the gaps created by winter losses in the herbaceous border, will not be in such good conditions, but the addition of a little fine peat or the contents of used growing bags scattered in such areas before sowing will enhance the chances of success.

Most gardeners consider April and May as the optimum months for sowing hardy annuals. However, it is wise to delay sowing until early June here in the north unless the spring is very early and the soil has warmed up. Little will be gained by sowing early on a cold uncompromising clay soil.

Seeds given these conditions often rot before they have an opportunity to germinate. It is important to regard sowing dates as a guide only, be influenced more by soil and weather conditions than the calendar.

Preparation of soil that has been weathered should be left until just prior to sowing. If a tilth is prepared too soon rain will compact the soil and spoil its structure. However, that is not to say that the soil should not be firmed before sowing. This can be done quite simply by shuffling across the bed with the feet after it has been knocked roughly level.

All that need be done afterwards is to create a shallow tilth with a rake. It is advisable to incorporate fertiliser at this stage, using a general kind applied at the rate recommended by the manufacturer for vegetable cultivation. Fertilisers like Growmore should only be used prior to sowing. Later applications can cause scorching of the foliage, particularly if the weather remains warm and dry.

When a border or bed is being planned exclusively for annuals, the sites can be marked out for the individual species and varieties with a sprinkling of sand. Groups of irregular shape and size always give the best effect. While taller kinds are usually better towards the back of the border or middle of the bed, strict regimenting is best avoided.

Annual seeds are usually covered with about their own depth of soil, large seeds such as nasturtiums being sown individually, while finer seed can be broadcast over its designated area and then raked in. The broadcasting of seed involves the even general distribution of seed by hand and using the eye to judge when it is sufficiently evenly spread. Very fine seeds that are difficult to distribute evenly should be mixed with a little dry silver sand. This enables the seed to be evenly dispersed and clearly shows the areas which have been covered.

In dry periods newly sown seed and emerging seedlings must be regularly watered to ensure that their growth continues unchecked. Crowded seedlings must be thinned at the first opportunity if damping off disease is to be avoided and strong healthy plants are to develop.

Special treatments

While the majority of seeds prefer warm equitable conditions in which to germinate freely, others depend upon chilling to break their dormancy. Yet many gardeners are reluctant to provide the necessary conditions for fear of damaging the seeds.

What happens in nature is that if conditions for germination are not amenable when the seed matures and falls to the ground, an embryo inhibitor acts to render the seed dormant until it has experienced a winter. This particularly applies to shade-loving plants like the Christmas rose which normally sheds its seed in dry summer conditions beneath the dense canopy of surrounding trees.

Germination cannot take place until the dry dusty conditions are moistened by winter rain and the leaf canopy is removed by autumn leaf fall. The indication to the seeds that conditions are favourable is freezing, which is quite obviously associated with that time of the year.

Winter has come with all its benefits and therefore frost effectively sends a message to the embryo which releases it from its dormancy. So the seeds should be sown in the normal way and the pans placed in a freezer for a week or ten days, subsequently being removed to a warm light environment, where germination will quickly follow.

Down-to-earth tip

There are some seeds that demand special treatment in order to give the best results. In the past gardeners have chipped hard coated seeds, notably those of the legume family, especially sweetpeas. These have very hard seed coats which are impervious to water and from which the embryo has great difficulty in breaking out. So gardeners have always taken sweetpea seeds and chipped their seed coats with a pen-knife in order to permit the absorbtion of water and to allow easy emergence of the young plant.

Each seed was examined, and at the end furthest from the scar where the seed was attached to the pod, a nick was made in the seed coat so that the white flesh of the seed could be seen. However it was not physically damaged by the cutting. This worked well, but it was obviously a very long and tedious exercise.

Following recent work with seeds of similar tropical legumes, a much simpler technique has been devised. If a sweetpea seed is observed under a microscope there will be evidence of a slight crazing of the seed coat. When this is enhanced moisture can be absorbed and the root can break out.

To create this enhancing of the crazing, place seeds to be chipped in a coffee or jam jar and shake them rhythmically for two minutes. The simplest way to do this is to count to 120 while shaking. Less than 120 may not cause sufficient enhancement, more than 120 may skin the seeds completely. Once this treatment is over the seeds can be sown in the usual fashion in pots or the open ground.

Propagation: Vegetative

There are many ways, apart from seed raising, of propagating garden plants.

Softwood cuttings

Most shrubby and herbaceous plants, as well as houseplants, can be increased from softwood cuttings. With flowering shrubs it is advisable to make cuttings from growth that is in a semi-ripe state. That is to say it is not soft and sappy, nor hard and woody, but of a greenish-brown or pinkish colour. Herbaceous and rock garden plants never produce growth of quite this texture. It is important that cuttings of any kind should always be young, robust and turgid.

The most satisfactory cuttings for all decorative plants are made from short pieces of healthy stem which are cut at a leaf joint. It is important that the base of the cutting is made at this point, for it is from here that the plant exhibits its greatest rooting potential. The only exception is clematis.

Always remove the lower leaves of the cutting as well as any that are likely to rest on the rooting medium and subsequently decompose. Large upper leaves can also be reduced in size by the careful use of the knife. This will further reduce moisture loss through transpiration.

Hormone rooting powders and liquids are invaluable aids in the propagation of a wide range of plants and the home gardener should make full use of them. All that is required is to dip the stem end of the cutting into the hormone preparation prior to insertion in the rooting medium. This will encourage root formation and prevent fungal infection

Use a rooting medium of equal parts sand and peat or perlite and peat, and keep

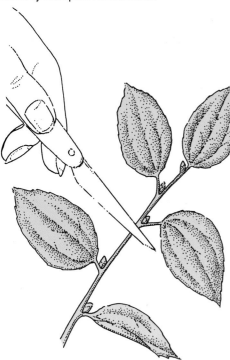

1 Cutting

Take cuttings from the leaf joint of a healthy stem.

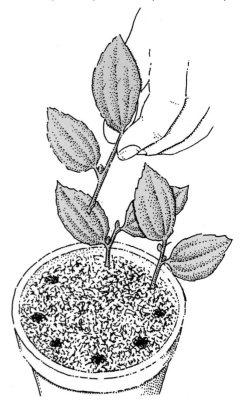

2 Planting

Plant cuttings around the edge of a pot of rooting medium.

the cuttings moist by regular overhead spraying with clear water. Rooting will then be rapid. Once the cuttings have started to root, lift them carefully and pot up individually in a good potting compost. The rooting medium has no nutrients in it and there is little benefit to be obtained from leaving them in it once roots have been initiated.

Spray freshly potted cuttings overhead regularly with clear water until they have become well established. This assists greatly in weaning them so that they can cope with the realities of life, especially when they have been raised in a closed propagator. If you do not have such luxury, the humidity of the kitchen creates an ideal atmosphere for all cuttings except those with grey or very hairy leaves.

Hardwood cuttings

Hardwood cuttings are used to propagate a wide range of shrubs and bush fruits. Whenever possible hardwood cuttings are selected from vegetative rather than flowering wood, taking care not to use thin pieces that are likely to dry out before rooting, nor stems that are thicker than a pencil, for these will be too old to root readily. Wood should be of the past summer's growth and be solid in cross-section. Hollow cuttings are most unlikely to root satisfactorily. In most cases suitable wood is of a light brown colour and full of the vigour of youth.

Lengths of stem about 9 ins. long are ideal. If the shrub is intended to have a leading growth, then the material should be selected from terminal shoots. If the shrub is to be bushy, then a length of stem can be cut into two or three pieces without you being concerned about a true terminal bud.

While the chances of rooting are enhanced by the use of a special medium, most popular woody subjects can be rooted directly outside in the open ground. It is important that the soil is in good condition and that the cut surface of the cutting makes firm contact with it.

It is usual to push the cutting into the soil for about half its length. However, before doing this decide whether the resulting shrub is intended to branch from the base or yield a shrub on a short stem or leg above the ground. If a shrub that is well branched from ground level is desired, then leave all the buds on the cutting when it is inserted. If a short clear stem is wanted, then all the lower buds must be removed to prevent suckering.

Layering

The same criteria for the selection of material applies for layers as for softwood cuttings, for the potential rooting problems are the same.

An incision should be made at a leaf joint. This should be made about half way through the stem and the cut surface pegged down to the soil with a wire staple.

Some gardeners prefer to sink pots of good potting compost or rooting medium into the ground around the parent plant and then peg layers directly into these. This has the advantage of providing a better medium for rooting and little disturbance is caused when the rooted layers are eventually detached from the mother plant.

The length of time that a cutting or layer takes to root varies from a few weeks to several months. As soon as rooting is detected the cuttings should be potted individually.

Division and root cuttings

Many plants are quite naturally divided during the course of their management. This is a form of propagation which is perhaps not always seen as such. However, if you wish to increase a particular alpine, herbaceous or aquatic plant it is not necessary to wait for it to become congested, it can be lifted and divided whenever it is seen to be divisible. Always use the outer, young, vigorous portions. Discard old woody material.

Some plants with fleshy roots, like oriental poppies and sea holly, can be increased from small pieces of healthy root. These should be about 1 in. long and no thicker than a pencil, but not so thin and stringy that they are likely to dry out.

Prepare these during the autumn and plant in a tray or pan of John Innes seed compost with about one third by volume of sharp sand added. Place in a cool sheltered place in the garden or in a cold frame. By the spring they should be sprouting and can then be potted up individually.

Paths, patios and walls

One of the banes of modern gardeners is the landscaper's use of hard landscape materials – bricks, concrete and paving. Many modern houses have the obligatory patio in place before the owner moves in, such is the belief that it is a must for everyone. Not that one should decry the patio, for properly constructed and sensibly sited it can be a delight. However, it is much better if with a new garden hard landscaping is not in place for then you have the option of choosing where walls, paths and other permanent features are constructed, for they are fairly immoveable, expensive to build and become rather tedious if situated incorrectly.

Paths

A well laid path is essential for the successful management of every garden. The direction that it takes must be very clearly thought through to ensure its efficiency. It must be arranged so that there are no temptations to cut corners across the lawn or flower beds and yet as far as possible it should be unobtrusive.

Like the garden itself, a path should be well drained, especially if it is to be constructed from gravel or a similar porous material. Surrounding ground must also be drained in such a fashion that the path does not become a water course during periods of heavy rain or after a snowmelt. The scouring out of gravel or hoggin by fast flowing ground water can be a considerable irritation.

Before construction, consider the possibility of the path also being the line which takes services. Water and electricity can very conveniently be taken along the line of the path so that there is never any danger of them interfering with cultivations. It would be ill-advised to place such services beneath a solid path, such as concrete, but ready access can be gained through a gravel or beneath a paved path.

A sound foundation is vital, even for a simple gravel path. If a generous layer of hardcore is not laid down first of all it is almost certain that mud will squeeze through and within a season the path will become a mud and gravel mixture. To some extent this can be prevented by using a fabric matting before spreading the gravel. While this will prevent mud from squeezing through it will not prevent humps and hollows.

There are all kinds of gravels and gravel-like materials which can be used for path construction, but all require a proper wooden or kerbed edging to retain the material. Many gardeners choose three quarter inch gravel as this is substantial and looks good. It is not the best utility choice though for it is quite difficult to push a wheelbarrow or pushchair on and it creates havoc for women wearing high heeled shoes.

Pea shingle is much finer and makes a far better surface providing that you do not scatter it too liberally. However the best of all is Breedon gravel. This is of gravel-like appearance but of such a texture that it binds together in a neat hard surface. Once laid it merely needs rolling with a garden roller. Runner crushed limestone can also serve the purpose, but it tends to become dusty during dry weather and pick up a bit on your shoes on wet days. It can also increase the alkalinity of nearby soil.

Concrete is a serviceable but harsh option which if laid properly with expansion

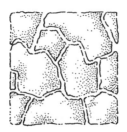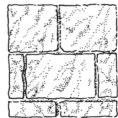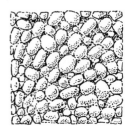

Patios and paths
From left; Herringbone, crazy paving, riven paving and cobbles

joints will last indefinitely. It is not a comfortable path to walk along or work from in hot weather as there is considerable reflection and glare. The same applies to some of the modern paving slabs made from reconstituted stone. Select these with great care choosing softer more subtle colours to reduce discomfort. Also carefully select the surface. There are a number of more or less non-slip surfaces available, the most natural looking of which is refered to as riven paving.

Patios

The comments made about paving for paths apply equally, if not more so, to patios. As a sitting out area, glare is going to be an even more important factor to take into consideration. Drainage, a sound foundation, and a level if perhaps slightly tilted surface to drain off rain water, are essential for a patio as well.

When deciding where the patio is to be situated take into account exposure, shade, sun and most important of all the view – although to some extent this is in the hands of the gardener. Of the elements, wind is unquestionably the one that causes the greatest discomfort so a sheltered spot is ideal.

A patio need not be a large paved area, so think carefully about all aspects of what for most people is an extension of the living room. A small pool may be desirable, or perhaps one or two beds, not necessarily in the ground, but raised to sitting level. Certainly where the patio runs up to a blank wall provision should be made to accommodate one or two climbing plants.

Patios are quite naturally places on which to stand tubs and planters. While this is fine for annuals and biennial bedding plants and bulbs, it is not so satisfactory for more permanent plants.

Within the relatively small confines of a tub or planter an ordinarily hardy climbing plant may fail. If the compost freezes solid the plant is likely to suffer root kill, or conversely during hot summer weather is going to be subjected to the possibility of drought and overheating. Most climbing plants enjoy their roots in the cool and shade and their heads in the sun and therefore are best in a border.

Walls

There are many kinds of wall construction, each of which should be the prerogative of an expert. Walls within the garden are expensive and usually confined to retaining soil. Wherever possible create a hollow wall in which plants can be grown to reduce its harshness.

There are many different materials from which walls can be constructed, brick and reconstituted stone being the most popular. However, there are often natural stone walls bounding a property and if these are in good order they can be made to appear more like garden walls than field divisions by adding plants.

Loose stone walls can often have plants with rootballs inserted into their crevices, but those that have been mortared or have tight joints are more difficult. To enable plants to become established it is possible to add seed to a mixture of wallpaper paste and peat and to smear this down the crevices. Plants like *Erimus* and *Asarina* are easily established this way.

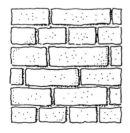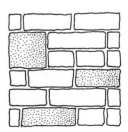

Walls
From left; English bond, dry stone, screen blocks and reconstituted stone.

Hedges and fences

Hedges and fences are necessary barriers for most gardens, not just delineating the boundaries of the property, but in many cases providing shelter. In fact many hedges are much more like screens or windbreaks, especially in northern gardens.

Screens and windbreaks

If your garden suffers exposure perhaps a windbreak should be considered rather than a hedge. Research has revealed that the best windbreak has five per cent porosity and that such a barrier will provide a relatively smooth flow of air with a minimum of turbulance and a speed reduction of over 30 per cent for a distance up to 30 times the height of the barrier.

Maximum effect though is for ten times the height of the barrier. Thus a 5 ft. barrier gives good effect for 50 ft. but a gradually reducing effect to 150 ft. In extremely exposed situations, or in gale force winds, this efficiency may be reduced by half. When a barrier of greater density is used, excessive turbulence is caused on the leeward side and the wind returns to its original speed far more quickly.

The length of a windbreak is also important, for if too short the wind is deflected around the ends and increased wind speeds occur at certain points. Gaps in a screen can lead to localised wind acceleration too.

Drainage of cold air from the site must not be impeded or frost damage will occur. This means that a screen must not be planted in a position which will cause cold air to remain in a pocket. Similarly when planting a windbreak across a slope it is recommended that the base of the trees be kept clear to allow cold air to flow down the slope.

Hedges

Although an essential part of almost every garden, hedges are invariably one of the most maligned and neglected features. The majority of gardeners just think of a hedge as a boundary marker which grows much too quickly and needs cutting incessantly.

This is unfortunate, for a well tended hedge that is treated as any other self-respecting plant would wish to be is a constant source of pleasure.

However, good hedges do not just happen, but come from careful soil preparation and choice of plants. This also applies to a living windbreak or screen.

Having decided upon the site for a hedge, mark out an area 3 ft. wide for its intended length. If the soil is very heavy and thought to be prone to water logging in the winter, then a tile drain or trench filled with old brickbats 2 ft. beneath the surface and leading to a soakaway will prove invaluable.

When the soil is poor, or perhaps subsoil, as is the case in many new gardens, then plenty of old well rotted manure, leaf mould or similar organic matter should be incorporated. Remember that this will be the last opportunity during the life of the hedge to get at the lower soil to enrich it.

Dig the area marked out and remove any weeds, especially perennials as these can quickly swamp young hedging plants. The upturned soil should be left to the mercy of

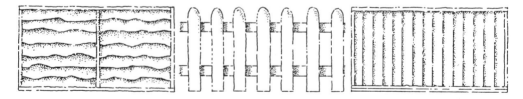

Fences

Require minimal maintenance and come in a variety of styles.

the elements before being broken down into a reasonable tilth ready for planting.

Planting

Planting of deciduous hedging plants can take place during autumn and winter but it is better to leave broad-leafed evergreens and conifers until late spring. Plants well furnished with foliage to ground level are ideal and are usually obtained more readily in smaller sizes. Large plants provide an instant barrier, but unless you are exceptionally lucky tend to have bare bases and seldom make a thick, impenetrable hedge.

Most hedging subjects are planted 12-18 ins. apart, generally in an alternate triangular fashion, although where space is very limited they sometimes have to be spaced out in a straight line.

Naturally the closer the planting the quicker the hedge will become serviceable, but if time is not a consideration a good hedge can be made more economically by spacing the plants slightly further apart and feeding them to encourage rapid growth.

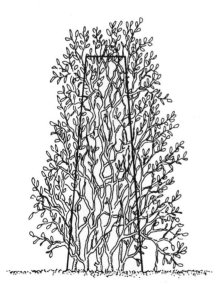

Hedges

Regular clipping is essential to keep the top narrower than the bottom.

Choosing a suitable subject for a particular purpose or situation is very important. Although most gardeners grow privet in either its green or golden form, there are equally amenable and often more suitable subjects for specific situations than those two old stalwarts.

For a boundary hedge the majority of commonly recommended hedging subjects are suitable, but where this adjoins fields that are likely to contain grazing cattle, yew, cupressus, thuya and most other conifers should be avoided. In this case thorn is the most satisfactory, making a rapid and impenetrable barrier. Holly, cherry and laurel are the least troublesome and most handsome of the popular evergreen hedging plants, but are relatively slow growing.

Green and copper beech make fine hedges, hanging on to their brown crisp leaves throughout the winter. Unfortunately they are a little fussy about soil and local conditions, so it is inadvisable to attempt them unless beech trees grow successfully in gardens and woodlands nearby.

Once successfully established, a young hedge requires considerable attention if it is to be an object of beauty in future years. It is always a mistake to let the plants grow too tall too quickly. Encourage dense bottom growth by keeping them low initially, otherwise they become top heavy and unwieldy and can only be rectified by drastic pruning. Regular clipping is essential, the object being to keep a narrower top than base in order to reduce the likelihood of snow damage during the winter.

Fences

Fences can serve the same purpose as hedges. Although often they are not so visually attractive, they have the advantage of taking nothing from the soil and requiring minimal maintenance. There are many different styles of fence from the low two rail ranch style through to the tall close boarded. The type that you use is a matter of personal taste. The most important factor is that it is well made and treated with a safe wood preservative. The fumes from creosote kills plants.

Lawn construction

A lawn can be created from either seed or turf. Both methods have their advocates and each demands a high standard of soil preparation. Drainage is absolutely vital, for a permanently wet or occasionally water-logged lawn will be plagued with moss. Ensure that drainage is installed for the lawn area in just the same way as for other parts of the garden.

The soil must be well cultivated and as far as possible troublesome perennial weeds should be removed. If you have time, allow the area to settle for a week or two. Any perennial weeds that are present should be allowed to begin to shoot and then can be treated with a glyphosate based systemic herbicide. This is much simpler than hand weeding.

The site should be levelled, any stones removed and then gently rolled. It is not vital for the lawn to be level from end to end and side to side, but it must be even and free from lumps and hollows. Remember that a seed raised lawn should have the soil level flush with any surrounding paths while one created from turf must allow for the thickness of the turf during preparation.

A lawn from seed

Usually the position of a lawn is determined by paths, buildings and other features so wherever possible choose a grass mixture that not only fulfils the requirements of the lawn that you desire, but which can cope with the often adverse conditions created by its situation.

A lawn that is going to be used for recreational purposes should be grown from a hard-wearing mixture containing rye grass. This is a coarse grass that is resilient and remains green even in times of adversity. An alternative to rye grass is the smooth-stalked meadow grass. Of similar habit, this cannot be cut as short as perennial rye, but it is particularly useful if the lawn is partially shaded.

A lawn that is intended primarily as a green backdrop for colourful borders and which will not receive heavy foot traffic should be composed of fine lawn grasses. These include chewing's fescue, creeping red fescue and brown top bent mixed in varying proportions. Creeping bent and vel-

vet bent are fine grasses which can also be considered if the soil conditions are good. Neither will tolerate a badly drained soil or extreme summer drought.

Trying to come up with your own mixture is very much a gamble unless you know your grass varieties well. It is more sensible to depend upon the judgement of the professional seedsman and use a commercially prepared mixture even if it costs a few pence more. Also be sure that your lawn seed, of whatever type, is treated with bird repellent. Seed is sown by hand, merely scattering it over the surface of the soil and then lightly raking in. Most mixtures are recommended for sowing at 2oz per sq yd, so for ease of working mark out squares that are approximately of a square yard each, running a cane along the soil to make marks. Measure out the appropriate amount of seed and get an egg-cup or cup that visually will provide an approximation of the amount being sown. This can be dipped into the bag and the contents distributed over each square.

Once the lawn has been sown it is very important to keep it well watered. Even when apparently well established, young grass can suffer very badly from drought.

A lawn from turf

Early autumn is the best time to establish a lawn from turf. If the grass can be laid before the onset of winter it will establish quickly and provide a usable lawn in spring.

The use to which the lawn is to be put will largely determine the type of turf that should be used. In recent years specific grass mixes have been sown to produce turf for particular purposes. A fine mixture for a purely decorative sward, a coarser mixture for the lawn that is to serve periodically as a football pitch. Never purchase what is popularly referred to as meadow turf. This can be anything. It may be good, but it is more likely to be infested with broad-leafed weeds and consist of a forage grass mixture.

Modern purpose grown turf is usually only marginally more expensive than pasture turf and has a consistent grass mixture throughout. The grasses from which it is comprised produce a tight network of roots

Laying turf

The individual lengths of turf should be laid in alternate rows like bricks in a wall

beneath the soil surface, which means that the turf can be lifted with a much thinner layer of soil than was previously possible.

Not only can purpose-grown turf be very accurately cut and lifted by machine, but it is also much lighter and easier to handle. Modern turf is so accurately cut that providing the soil beneath is level, the resulting lawn will also be level. In order to even out any discrepancies in the surface and to aid more rapid rooting, it is useful to spread a thin layer of river sand over prepared soil.

The individual lengths of turf should be laid in alternate rows in the same pattern that is used for bricks in a wall. Lay the first row in a straight line, even if the edge of the lawn is curved. The curved area can be filled later. It is most important that turf Is laid from a fixed straight line.

Push each piece close to the next. Once an area has been laid brush sand into the cracks. This all helps the turf to knit to-

gether. Use a light roller to firmly press the turf to the soil and ensure maximum contact. At this stage if you need to stand on the lawn, only do so on a plank of wood.

If the weather becomes dry, water the turf freely. Once turf has shrunk it never joins back together again successfully. When turf is established during the autumn it rarely needs cutting before the winter. If a light cut becomes inevitable, set the mower blades as high as possible.

Down-to-earth tip

When watering a lawn it is difficult to know how much water you have applied. Before switching on the sprinkler, place a jam jar underneath its spread. This will collect water and will indicate how much you have provided. It is much better than guessing from the feel of the turf how much water is there.

Lawn maintenance

The regular care and maintenance of the lawn is vital. It is the lawn which is usually the centrepiece of the garden.

Mowing and edging

Correct mowing is very important for the maintenance of a good sward. Leave the grass to get too long and the mower will start to cause damage. Finer grasses will disappear and coarser kinds will take over.

The close cutting of turf is equally damaging, the grass being affected by dry weather, dying out and giving an opportunity for moss to become established. Close cutting can also lead to surface scalping, which not only creates bare patches, but damages the lawn mower.

To ensure a first class cut on a lawn composed of fine grasses, a cylinder mower is essential. The more blades that the cutting cylinder has, the finer the cut. Rotary cutters are best for banks and longer tougher grass but do not give such a fine finish. They rarely have the facility for gathering cut material, but this is of little consequence providing that the cuttings are not excessive and are spread around evenly.

The maintenance of a neat edge is vital if a lawn is going to look good all year round. During summer this merely consists of cutting off excess leafy growth with edging shears every time you mow the grass.

It is essential that the edges being trimmed are clean cut so that the shears can rest against them and make a neat job. The edge should slope back a little so that when you walk near to it the turf does not break away. If edges are vertical or slightly undercut this can cause a problem, especially on lighter soils.

To cut a good edge it is necessary to use an edging iron with a flat blade of half moon shape. Placed against a straight edge like a scaffold board, it is simple to make a neat clean cut. A strong garden line can also be used. This is vital for curves and arcs.

Weeding and watering

The maintenance of a good lawn depends upon the control of weeds. Broad leafed weeds of all kinds provide competition for the grass and spoil the overall appearance of an even green sward. It is important to control weeds from the time that the lawn is established. Use a translocated weedkiller.

This is one that is absorbed by the foliage and moves throughout the sap stream of the plant.

Remember that after applying weedkiller to the lawn it is unwise to use the first two collections of lawn mowings on the compost heap. They may be tainted and cause problems in the garden later.

Watering is essential for the establishment of a new lawn, whether it is being grown from seed or turf. Seedling grass is vulnerable to drying out, while turf shrinks during hot weather and leaves gaping cracks in the surface which are impossible to close.

With a new lawn it is vital to water before damage occurs, but with an established sward you have more leeway. A brown lawn will generally return to green after sustained watering, but it is never as good and usually becomes invaded by moss.

Autumn care

Much can be done during the autumn to rejuvenate and prepare the lawn for its winter vigil. Providing that soil conditions are moist, the preparations that are made during the autumn will pay dividends in the spring. Bare patches are common at this time of the year. These can be caused by compaction of the soil, competition from moss or weeds, or scalping with the lawn mower. Scalping is common when the lawnmower plate has been set too low and the surface of the lawn is uneven. There is no reason to cut the grass so short that scalping becomes a regular occurence, but occasionally part of the lawn may need levelling if the mower catches it frequently. It is a simple matter to lift the offending area of turf, remove some soil from beneath, and then replace.

Compaction can give rise to an invasion by moss because the soil becomes stagnant, especially after a period of wet weather. More commonly though, bare patches are damp, smeared areas of turf which arise from children's cricket creases and goal mouths, where the grass has just been worn away completely.

In this case, and also where moss has been a nuisance, it is essential to aerate the damaged area with a hollow tined fork before attempting rejuvenation. A generous application of sharp sand should then be applied to help keep the soil open and free-draining.

Irrespective of how bare patches have occured, it is essential for the re-establishment of a sward to lightly cultivate the damaged areas prior to re-sowing with a mixture of grass seed and a soil based compost such as John Innes No.1. Specific lawn repair kits known as 'reseeders' are available. When one of these is used, the soil on the area to be treated should be broken up to a fine tilth, the reseeder scattered over, and then covered with moist peat or sifted garden soil.

Different grades are available according to whether the lawn is decorative or functional. It is important that you select the correct kind. Also if you are purchasing a seed mixture it is vital that you have the same constituent grasses as the original lawn.

During autumn it is essential to remove fallen leaves from grass. Apart from encouraging the activities of earthworms, fallen leaves that remain untouched for several days will cause yellowing of the grass beneath. Regular raking with a spring tine rake is essential. Apart from gathering up the leaves, the scarifying stimulates the turf and disperses worm casts.

Spring care

Providing that autumn care has been carried out thoroughly, all that is required in the spring is an application of a lawn weed and feed product. After a very wet winter it is useful to aerate the turf again.

1 Aerating
Use a hollow tined fork to aerate the turf after a wet winter and before attempting to rejuvenate damaged areas of the lawn.

2 Scarifying
Regular raking is essential in the autumn to remove fallen leaves, stimulate turf and disperse worm casts.

Tree selection

When purchasing a tree never do so on impulse. Always consider the various attributes of each species or variety – its size, colour, shape and the position it will occupy in your garden. Trees can grow to a great height and completely swamp a small garden. Find out the ultimate height and shape of the tree. Do you want one that is tall, upright, round headed, weeping, prostrate or low branched? The choice is infinite.

Different soil types support some trees better than others. Acidity or alkalinity, soil texture and drainage all have a bearing upon the kind of tree that will grow best.

Making a choice

Modern gardens are generally small and do not readily lend themselves to trees of a traditional kind. However, there are a number of fastigiate or upright growing varieties which can be successfully accommodated in very confined spaces. Fastigiate trees are in effect freaks of nature. Instead of spreading their branches in the usual fashion they have a tight, upright columnar growth but with all the other characteristics of their cousins. There are fastigiate forms of many trees from oaks to flowering cherries, but one of the most impressive is the upright variety of beech called Dawyck.

Many trees are naturally of diminutive stature and a single specimen can often be successfully accommodated on a small town plot. But it is then important to select a tree that will give as much value as possible. Some of the maples are excellent, with attractive marbled and peeling bark and handsome foliage that takes on fiery autumnal tints. The purple leafed plum and weeping silver leafed pear are also excellent value, as well as some of the decorative crab apples which provide edible fruits.

Rowans, whitebeams, flowering cherries

The sorbus are amongst the most startling groups of trees for the modern garden. They embrace the rowan or mountain ash as well as the whitebeam. The rowans have leaves with numerous leaflets, while the whitebeam types are typified by simple toothed or lobed leaves, often with a greyish bloom. Our native mountain ash is an excel-

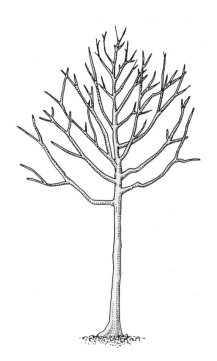

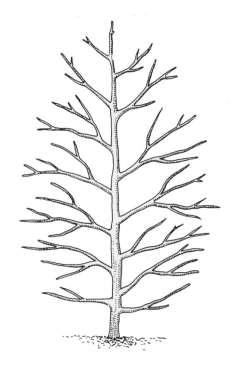

lent tree, with fresh green divided leaves, bold clusters of creamy-white blossoms and large bunches of orange or red fruits. It can be a little over-powering in the smaller garden where it is best replaced by the upright growing Sheerwater Seedling.

The laciniate rowan, or Asplenifolia, is an elegant tree with deeply cut fernlike foliage while the variety Xanthocarpa has regular leaves and fruits of rich orange-yellow. Joseph Rock is another popular kind. It has creamy-yellow fruits and in autumn has the most magnificent crimson-purple foliage.

Whitebeams are represented by our native *Sorbus aria* and its progeny. A widespread inhabitant of chalklands in southern Britain, it is an excellent tree for the north with a compact dome-shaped head of grey-green foliage and bold clusters of deep red waxy-looking fruits. The golden-leafed variety Chrysophylla has magnificent foliage, but a less pleasing habit. Pendula has a lovely weeping shape.

Of all the garden trees, ornamental cherries are amongst the most useful. Not just the flowering cherries, with which most gardeners are familiar, but species that have other qualities as well. *Prunus serrula* is one of the stars of the family, being planted for its incredible bark, which for most of the year is like polished red-brown mahogany. Against a clear blue sky and backdrop of snow this provides one of the most spectacular sights in the garden during winter. It flowers as well, tiny white blossoms like delicate snow-flakes sprinkled amongst its willowy green foliage.

Attractive bark is also one of the virtues of Sargent's cherry together with its myriad bright pink blossoms and rich red and orange autumnal colour. One of the best small cherries for the modern garden, it is surpassed only by the icing sugar-pink Japanese cherry Kanzan. With upright branches smothered in fully double pink blossoms towards the end of April, it makes a spectacular show. Only Shirotae can offer any challenge. This broad spreading tree of traditional Japanese appearance becomes laden with semi-double, papery, white blossoms that reverberate with the hum of bees throughout late April and early May.

The decorative cherries grow well on rich heavy soils, especially those that are alkaline. Light soils should be improved with plenty of organic matter. Species which are cultivated for their decorative bark and all the popular kinds of Japanese flowering cherry should be grown as standards or half-standards for the best effect.

What to look for

Traditional nurserymen who grow open ground plants and lift and sell them directly to the public are few and far between now, but if you do have one in your area you would be well advised to patronise him.

Irrespective of where you purchase your tree there are a number of golden rules to observe. The first concerns its general health and well being. Obvious signs of disease or pest damage shows neglect. While most will not be transmissible to the garden during the dormant season, it is wise to avoid establishments that do not have a good record of hygiene.

Grafted plants should also be carefully inspected to see that a sound union has been made. A weak union cannot be readily strengthened. It is also useful to know about the rootstock. Modern rootstocks are very consistent, often named, and sometimes seen noted on the labels of grafted plants.

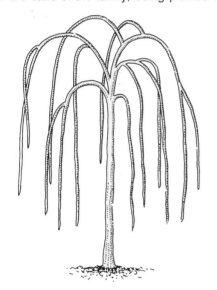

Tree shapes
From left, standard, feathered and weeping

Tree planting and care

A tree is a permanent feature within a garden, in most cases being likely to outlive the planter. It is therefore vital that proper provision is made for its development over many years.

Container grown trees

Nowadays most trees are grown in containers and are available for planting at most seasons of the year. It is not always ideal to plant at any season, but the facility is there, and unless the ground is frozen solid, trees can be established at any period given proper aftercare.

Composts in which container grown trees are planted are properly balanced to ensure their satisfactory development. Providing that feeding with a suitable fertiliser is continued during its life in the container, a tree grown in this manner is likely to be better able to become established in your garden than one lifted directly from a field.

There are limits to the period of containerised growth though, for long established woody plants do sometimes demand radical root pruning if they have remained in the same pot for three of four years.

Such plants will not be found in well ordered garden centres, but there are many pot bound specimens about. The roots grow in a spiral fashion around the container and become woody and corkscrew-like. They are then reluctant to break out into the surrounding soil.

To overcome this problem, any tree that is purchased in such a condition should be removed from its container and the rootball broken open. This can only be undertaken successfully during the dormant season, it should never be chanced in the summer months.

If a generous amount of tree and shrub planting compost is incorporated at planting time, the tree should become established without too much difficulty.

Any tree that is purchased from a garden centre and has obviously spent too long in its container is under stress. So if you have to purchase such a tree, bear this in mind and tend it carefully for a substantial period after planting.

Bare rooted trees

With the established rootball produced in a container, a tree has an excellent chance of rooting into the surrounding soil and growing away quickly, compared with an ordinary bare-rooted tree which has no hold on the soil and has to start ramifying the soil with its roots right from scratch. That is not to say that bare-rooted trees are not a good buy, for in some cases they are necessary or preferable. If you want a particular variety and have to order it from a specialist mail order nursery, then obviously it is likely to be uneconomical to send it in a pot full of heavy compost. It is also possible for the home gardener to purchase larger specimens grown in the open ground than are usually available from containers.

Planting

Open ground trees are planted during the dormant winter period. Container grown trees can be planted at any time given suitable aftercare. Evergreens are normally planted during September or March.

When planting ensure that the hole is large enough to accommodate all the roots when they are spread out, and that the soil in the bottom of the hole is broken up. It is also important to put the stake in the hole at the same time as the tree so that damage to the roots can be avoided.

In order to encourage the rapid formation of life-giving hair roots, add tree planting compost and spread this in and amongst the roots. Then replace the soil and firm it around the tree, ensuring that the final soil level corresponds with the mark on the stem which indicates the depth at which the tree was growing in the nursery.

Secure the tree to the stake with proper tree ties and keep an eye on it throughout the winter, especially during the severe weather. Frost disturbs newly planted trees and shrubs, so after a prolonged cold spell it may be necessary to firm the soil around the roots again.

If you are transplanting such a tree, unless it is a rather small specimen, it is preferable to dig around it during the summer before transplanting. This cuts the main roots and encourages the tree to develop a fibrous root system.

When the tree is lifted in the autumn a sizeable rootball can be secured which will enable re-establishment without difficulty. Although not vital, summer preparation does ensure greater success, especially with larger specimens.

After care

It is likely that the majority of gardeners will plant trees that have been grown in containers. While in ideal conditions they grow away quickly, it often happens that the weather turns against us and our soil conditions are perhaps not quite what we thought. High winds and a heavy clay soil, for example, make particular demands upon the newly planted tree, but the precautions taken under these rather extreme conditions are wise for any gardener with a newly planted tree to consider.

For most gardeners it is the roots of the trees that are the primary concern. This is quite reasonable given that it is roots that are responsible for the transporting of moisture and nutrients into the plant. However, in the summer we must not neglect the actively transpiring leaf canopy. The leaves transpire and give up moisture to the air at the same rate irrespective of whether the tree or shrub is well established, so we should seek to reduce this loss at such a critical time in the young plant's life.

Until recently we have shown little concern about moisture loss through transpiration and generally disregarded its debilitating effect. Not that anything could be done about it anyway.

It is the advent of an American anti-transpirant spray that has changed all this. A colourless spray, when it dries it covers the leaf surfaces with a clear, flexible film which does not affect any other plant functions but transpiration. So now it is possible to plant leafy trees and shrubs in the middle of summer without fear of wilting and with every expectation of rapid establishment. For the best results plants should be thoroughly soaked with water two or three hours before planting and then sprayed with the product. Ensure that both underside and upper leaf surface are properly covered.

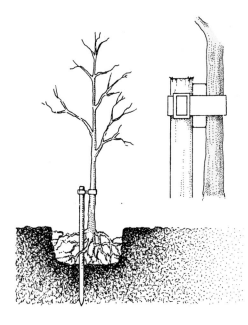

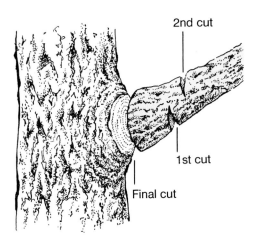

Removing branches

Reduce the weight of the branch by removing most of it before the final cut.

2nd cut

1st cut

Final cut

Staking

The buckle-adjustable tie is nailed at the top of the stake to prevent it slipping.

Flowering shrubs

There are few gardens that would not be improved by the addition of one or two decorative shrubs. Indeed for the busy gardener they are ideal, requiring the minimum of attention and being capable of providing colour and interest the whole year through.

Winter colour

Even in the depths of winter a dark corner can be brightened by the lovely *Mahonia bealei*. Of upright growth, this gorgeous subject produces densely packed sprays of bright yellow blossoms from November until February. The variety Charity is exceptional and a prime choice for the northern garden.

The witch hazel makes a good companion, its delicate clusters of richly fragrant golden blossoms being borne on naked branches and standing defiant against the most severe winter weather. A selected form called Goldcrest is even more lovely, its slender petals being suffused with deep crimson.

Daphne mezereum is a good companion, being of modest growth and with leafless branches that during February and March are garlanded with purple blossoms. These are sweetly scented and followed during late summer by clusters of scarlet berries.

Spring flowers

The forsythia, its boughs laden with delicate golden bells, heralds the arrival of spring. Modern varieties like Lynwood Gold and Beatrix Farrand produce large blossoms of a vivid hue and there is now a miniature variety called Arnold's Dwarf which is well suited to the smaller garden.

Flowering currants, with their pendant clusters of rose-pink blooms, make a useful contrast and provide colour from April until the middle of May. The common kind is a lusty fellow of considerable merit, but the rich crimson King Edward VII and deep red Pulborough Scarlet are exceptional.

The various brooms are much underrated shrubs and are especially useful for dry inhospitable situations in full sun. What is more, they are available in almost every shape, size and colour imaginable.

Viburnums are essentially late spring and summer flowering shrubs which are mostly very fragrant and reliable. *Viburnum burkwoodii* is amongst the most popular, but the snowball bush, *V.opulus* Sterile and (V.) Lanarth follow a close second.

Summer shrubs

Mock orange or Philadelphus are very reliable and come in all shapes and sizes, although the blossoms are always white and heavily scented. *Philadelphus* Virginal is a lovely double form that flowers well even as a small shrub, while *P.coronarius* has single blossoms which in its variety Aureus are beautifully set off by golden-green foliage.

Hydrangeas are good standbys for windswept gardens, growing especially well beside the sea. In addition to the pink, blue and white common kinds there are some beautiful varieties with mop-heads or lace-cape flowers. There is also a climbing kind and one with soft downy foliage.

Grey leaves are the major attraction of *Senecia laxifolius*, another good shrub for exposed places. This also has bright yellow daisy-like flowers and prospers in hot sunny spots in impoverished soil. On a heavy rich soil it often produces lush foliage that rarely survives our cold damp winters.

The Californian lilacs or ceanothus are most accommodating and can be planted in varieties that will flower from spring until late summer. They normally occur in shades of blue, but there are both white and pink varieties too. All require a sunny situation and appreciate the protection of a wall.

Autumn blossoms

Autumn flowering shrubs are few and far between, but many produce attractive fruits and brilliant autumn colour. The innumerable varieties of berberis are of immense value in this respect, all bearing decorative berries and a number having foliage that takes on delightful autumnal tints.

The firethorn or pyracantha is also noted for its fruits. A splendid evergreen that drips clusters of orange, red or yellow berries, it is a most versatile character, being amenable to training as a wall shrub. Nowadays flowering and decorative shrubs can be planted all the year around, providing they have been grown in containers. During the summer months they need regular watering to ensure successful establishment. This even applies to those planted in damp conditions during spring.

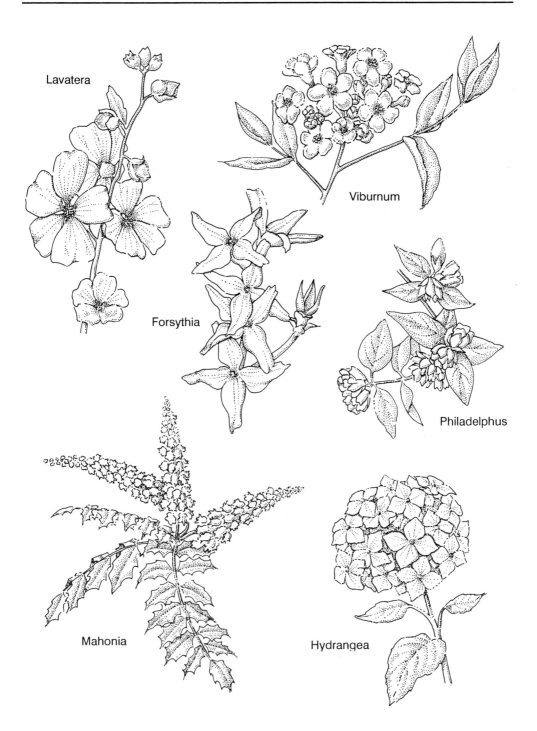

Lavatera

Viburnum

Forsythia

Philadelphus

Mahonia

Hydrangea

Evergreens and conifers

Broad-leafed evergreen shrubs and conifers form the backbone of the garden, especially during winter. While having a reputation for being dull and uninteresting, this is nowadays unjustified, for modern varieties are available in almost every shape and size imaginable and in brilliant shades of green, blue, grey and gold.

Planting

Evergreens should be planted during early autumn, this gives them an opportunity to settle in and make some root growth before the onset of severe weather. Planted later they will often just sit inactively in wet soil and run the risk of suffering water-logging.

Spring planting is not as satisfactory because the soil is still cold following winter and neither evergreens nor conifers are encouraged to make rapid root development. This, coupled with the fact that during March we often experience cold drying winds, means that even though the winter is in prospect, evergreens planted during early autumn have a much better chance of becoming established.

Most evergreens transplant readily from open ground as they make nice fibrous root systems. The only exceptions are the conifers with needles, like pine, fir and spruce. These have rather wiry roots which do not hold soil readily, so when you are buying this kind of conifer select a container grown specimen rather than one from open ground. This will have a much better chance of establishment.

Evergreens

There are innumerable broad-leafed evergreen shrubs, some of which are grown merely for their foliage, others for either fruits or flowers. One of the favourites for the northern garden is holly.

Holly is tolerant of most situations, although it will not prosper on a severely alkaline soil. There are very many clones of the common holly, some of which have strong ties with tradition, others that are rather bizarre and scarcely recognisable as holly. There is an extraordinary variety called J.C.

Van Tol with leaves that are a dark glossy green and almost spineless, its regular crops of red fruits being the only clue that it is a true holly.

Or at the other extreme there is Ferox with its viciously spined leaves, an old-fashioned robust sort that can be highly commended for hedging too. Its cream and gold blotched forms known as Ferox Argentea and Ferox Aurea look even more fierce. All are male trees and so produce no berries.

When this is the case it is always profitable to go for a variegated clone. These are able to pollinate the female clones and so ensure berries. There is no reason to persist with a dull green male when a variegated holly can be grown.

Another one worth considering is a variety known as Golden Queen. Despite a name which suggests otherwise, this is a male. Conversely the variety called Golden King is a female. This fruits profusely with bunches of orange-red berries.

Laurel is another sound evergreen, the common *Prunus laurocerasus* growing under conditions of sun or shade in either damp or dry soil. There are named varieties with lower growing or more compact growth, the popular Otto Luyken producing attractive candles of creamy flowers too.

Conifers

Conifers come in a wide range of shapes and sizes, from towering redwoods to creeping junipers. But in between are a host of beautiful evergreens in a variety of forms and colours which provide interest all the year round.

The cypresses are the most important group. Most of us are familiar with the ubiquitous hedging and screening Lawson's cypress. It is from this that numerous attractive and colourful varieties have been derived for use in groups or as single specimens.

Conifers not only rely upon colour for effect, but depend heavily upon shape and form. Those like the glaucous Columnaris and rich green Erecta Viridis have a spire-like habit. Wisselii has dense clusters of foliage and twisting branches, while Forsteckensis grows into a big green ball.

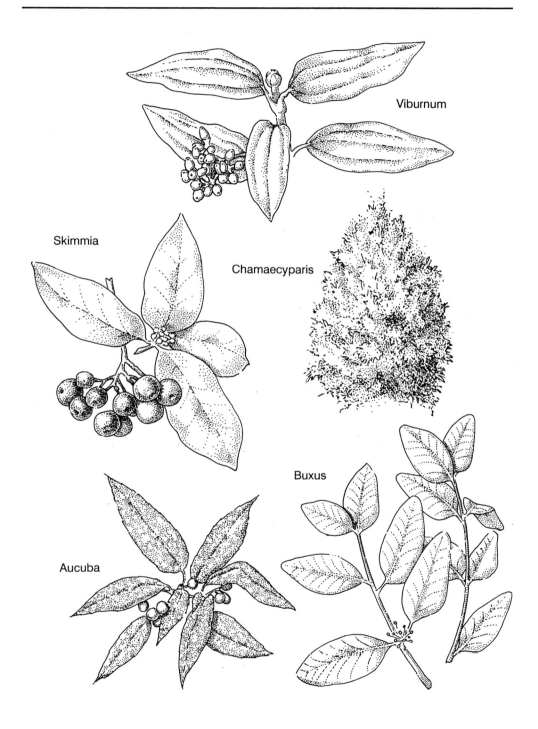

Viburnum

Skimmia

Chamaecyparis

Buxus

Aucuba

Climbing and wall plants

Climbing plants are those that depend upon another for support. In the wild they often grow in hedgerows or amongst the under-storey of deciduous woodlands.

Not all climbing plants are perennial or even woody. Some, like the morning glories or ipomaeas, are annuals. Others such as the flame flower, Tropaeolum speciosum, are perennial, but herbaceous, and die right down to the ground during the winter.

In garden terms many trees and shrubs that benefit from the protection of a wall are loosely classified as climbers, even though they are not self-supporting.

Clematis

Clematis are extremely versatile, being ideal for clothing fences, walls, arbours or even old fruit trees. However, they must have sun. Clematis will not prosper and flower freely in a gloomy corner.

Not that sun is everything, for clematis are naturally hedgerow plants where they have their heads in the sun and roots in the shade. Where such conditions can be pro-vided they are amongst the easiest climbers to grow.

It is not often practical to reproduce ex-actly the conditions of a hedgerow, but as long as the principles are followed closely then few problems will arise.

The shaded base need not be provided by dwarf shrubs like potentilla, although this is usually more natural and presentable.

A paving slab placed over the soil in the immediate vicinity of the root system is equally effective in providing a cool root run.

Soils present few difficulties, for clematis can grow with equal indifference whether it be heavy or light, although the extremes of either are likely to prove debilitating. Very acid land is not appreciated, but chalky soils are loved.

Planting young plants from containers is the ideal, never be tempted by those large, bulky plants sometimes seen at garden cen-tres with roots hanging all out of their pots. These can be established successfully, but require an infinite amount of care.

When planting close to a building, take heed of the likely extent of the foundations, for these may restrict root development.

The overhang of the roof must also be considered as this can effect the availability of moisture. Where either of these problems are likely to arise, then apply a generous mulch of well rotted garden compost in the spring to conserve moisture.

Choosing varieties

The diversity of clematis is such that they can be used in almost any role. Modern hy-brids are excellent for clothing walls and fences. Species like *Clematis montana* will happily festoon an old fruit tree or cover an outhouse, while the non-clinging *C. durandii* will trail as well as scramble.

For the majority of gardeners it is the large flowered kinds that hold the greatest

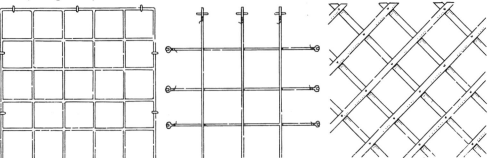

Plant supports
From left; Stapled galvanized chain link, stretched line wires fixed with eyes and prefabricated trellis cut to fit and pinned onto posts.

attraction. Bold, starry blossoms in almost every colour imaginable and in varieties that will start flowering during May and carry on until August.

Two of these are widely grown and loved by all gardeners: Jackmanii Superba and Nelly Moser. The former is a July flowering kind with deep purple flowers while the latter is more refined, with an extended flowering season and beautifully sculptured blossoms of mauve with a conspicuous lilac bar.

Ville de Lyon is carmine red, Duchess of Edinburgh has double flowers of cool icy-white and Ernest Markham is rich magenta. Lincoln Star has raspberry-pink flowers, Richard Pennell blossoms of deepest lavender and Proteus lilac-rose and fully double, like an old fashioned paeony.

Of the species, the May blooming *C. montana* is unquestionably the most popular. An easy going plant of vigorous habit with myriad small creamy-white blossoms. There are several forms including the pink flowered Rubens, rich rose-pink Tetrarose and fragrant soft pink Elizabeth.

These are all boisterous climbers that benefit from having their main stems tied to their support to prevent them being blown down in high winds.

Unlike the large flowered hybrids that require a strict pruning regime, *C. montana* and its progeny are merely tidied up each year and kept within bounds.

Most gardeners find pruning clematis a complicated subject, but in very general terms it can be simplified.

With large flowered hybrids it is a question of pruning early flowering ones down to the ground after blossoming to enable them to produce wood during the summer that will yield flowers next year.

Those that do not come into bloom until well into the summer flower on the current season's growth and therefore need cutting to the ground in early spring.

Most natural species, although given a definite pruning sequence in most gardening books, are best left to their own devices. Just keep them within bounds and remove dead, dying or weak growths.

Other climbers

Honeysuckles are grown primarily for their refreshing sweet fragrance and there are none better than the varieties of Japanese honeysuckle, *Lonicera japonica*. Halliana bears snow-white blossoms which age to sulphurous yellow, while Aureoreticulara has leaves that are variegated green and gold. Old-fashioned Dutch honeysuckles, *L. periclymenum* Belgica and Serotina, have striking cream flowers flushed with purple, while the evergreen *Lonicera henryi* sports rich yellow blooms splashed and stained with crimson.

Wisteria, with its long chains of lilac blossoms, is a constant source of delight in early summer. The Chinese *Wisteria sinensis* is the one most frequently encountered, but its white form Alba and dark purple variety Black Dragon are worthy of consideration.

Autumn colour can be provided by the foliage of decorative vines like the brilliant scarlet *Vitis pulchra* and rich purple *V. amurensis*. But *V. coignetiae* is king of them all, with immense heart-shaped leaves that turn vivid red and dense pendant clusters of tiny black grapes.

If you are looking for something quite outstanding, especially if you are confronted with a north-facing wall, try the climbing hydrangea, *Hydrangea petiolaris*. This aimiable character will cover a wall in fresh green foliage and as soon as spring turns to summer will start producing an abundance of glistening white lace-cap type blossoms that will continue well into August. Being self clinging it is very easy to accommodate in most situations.

Garrya elliptica is another good plant for a tricky north-facing position. An evergreen, it is not climbing but free-standing yet benefits from being grown in such a position. Although not spectacular, it is very useful, producing long greenish-grey catkins during the depths of winter, a perfect companion for that other January blooming wall plant the winter jasmine, *Jasminum nudiflorum*. This rather untidy character will lighten the darkest days with its slender green stems wreathed in starry lemon coloured blossoms.

Ground cover

Ground cover is every gardener's idea of an easy life. Plant suitable subjects and they will grow together, suppress weeds, and provide trouble-free colour for years to come. While eventually part of this dream can become a reality, it does not happen without careful planning.

Ground cover plants do not all grow conveniently at the same rate, nor at the same density, so variable planting distances are necessary. These distances should also be varied according to the speed with which the soil is to be covered.

With many varieties denser planting can ensure quicker cover. Care must be taken though, for some plants eventually produce a lumpy visual effect if they are planted too closely and are unable to develop naturally.

A number of shrubby ground cover plants are excellent for smothering the soil, but grow rather taller than might be expected. This is particularly true with some of the low growing cotoneasters and junipers which may attain 3ft or more in height.

Soil conditions

The soil is the most vital component in the successful establishment of a ground cover feature. This may seem to be obvious, for everyone knows that soil structure, and consequently drainage, makes a big difference to the ability of various plants to prosper, so too does the pH value – whether the soil is acid or alkaline.

Most gardeners hope to create a smooth, even carpet of foliage with ground cover plants. However, the majority forget that in order to do this the soil conditions must be uniform throughout the area to be planted. Even the proximity of a drain or old foundation near the soil surface can cause radical differences in the rate of growth, so can the presence of sub-soil.

Strive to ensure that there is at least a spade's depth of soil throughout.

Planting

Although dense planting will mostly ensure rapid cover it does not always yield the best long term results. Ground cover planted at distances that will give uniform soil coverage in a period of no more than three to four years is usually longer lived and better looking than crowded planting.

Establishment

During establishment weeds are likely to be troublesome. Mulching with composted bark, gravel or polythene mulch will assist. However, some weeds will appear and must be dealt with swiftly and regularly. If allowed to seed in establishing ground cover plants they will be a constant source of trouble.

Little maintenance is required during the development stage. Straggling shoots or stray branches may need removing and when some plants like heaths and heathers have finished flowering it is prudent to trim them back with shears.

Once ground cover is well established it should be fed. Use a general fertiliser during the spring. Do not over do the application. Aim for stable growth rather than rapid extension for tight, dense, foliage cover.

Plant selection

For tough shaded conditions in a cold climate the periwinkles are difficult to beat. The lesser periwinkle, *Vinca minor* produces bright blue starry flowers for much of the summer. It has white and purple flowers as well as variegated foliage varieties. The greater periwinkle *Vinca major* has large blue blossoms and more substantial foliage.

Rose of Sharon, *Hypericum calycinum*, is another first class evergreen ground cover for harsh conditions. Throughout the summer its handsome foliage is littered with bright golden blossoms four inches across. *Hypericum moseranum* is a much more orderly but slightly taller hybrid with smaller yellow flowers with conspicuous orange-red anthers.

Creeping Jenny, *Lysimachia nummularia*, is one of the finest ground cover plants for a damp or dingy corner. A ground hugging semi-evergreen with bright yellow buttercup-like blossoms. The variety Aurea is quite extraordinary with foliage that is almost as vivid a yellow as its blossoms.

The bugles or ajugas enjoy similar conditions. These will form dense carpets of colourful foliage amongst which spikes of bright blue flowers appear during summer. There are innumerable varieties with colourful foliage, but the dark reddish-purple Burgundy and multicoloured Rainbow are amongst the best.

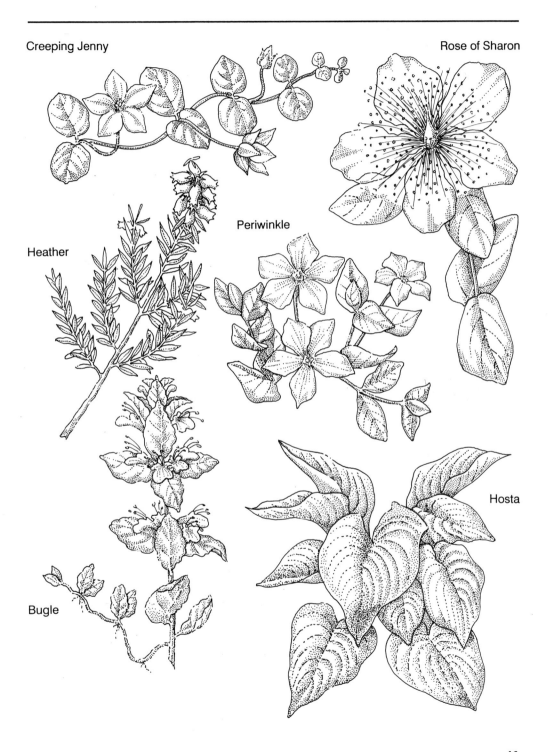

Creeping Jenny

Rose of Sharon

Heather

Periwinkle

Bugle

Hosta

Herbaceous plants and annuals

Herbaceous plants are those that die down annually and mostly reappear the following year. In gardeners' terms herbaceous plants are perennials, although botanically both annuals and biennials are of an herbaceous nature. With the trend towards smaller gardens, the day of the pure herbaceous border is virtually over. Most gardeners now content themselves with a mixed planting, often a combination of border perennials and hardy annuals.

Herbaceous plants

When growing herbaceous perennial plants, good soil preparation cannot be over emphasised. It is likely to be several years before the plants are lifted and divided again, therefore the opportunity to incorporate organic matter into the soil and generally improve its structure should be taken whenever the border is vacant.

Perennial weeds like thistles, bindweed and couch grass should be eliminated before planting. If allowed to invade the border they become impossible to get rid of, becoming entangled in the roots of desirable herbaceous plants and providing a permanent reservoir of infestation.

Hand picking of perennial weeds is useful, but more certain results can be obtained by the use of a weed killer containing the active ingredient glyphosate. If sprayed onto the vigorous young leafy growth of weeds this is translocated throughout the sap stream and kills the plant entirely without polluting the soil. Even bits of root that might be missed by hand picking succumb to this treatment if sprouting.

A rich organic soil is ideal for herbaceous plants and therefore the incorporation of copious amounts of old rotted manure or garden compost is vital. A general fertiliser can be distributed prior to planting and will result in improved growth.

There is very little difference between planting a new border and replanting an existing one but an existing border may well have clumps of perennials in it that resent disturbance and these must be worked around. Border plants like paeonies and Christmas roses should rarely be lifted as

they take so long to re-establish. Lupins, and any other members of the pea family, have to be increased by seed or cuttings as they do not move or divide well.

Once the soil is prepared the marking out for groups of plants can be done. It is useful to have a sketch on paper of what is intended, but do not be too dogmatic about its application. Herbaceous plants should always be planted in groups, never attempt to plant single plants as the effect is not then one of a harmonious border, but of a stamp collection. Border plants need to be grown in groups of three, five or seven.

Within reason, the larger the group the better. To help create suitable arrangements, scatter sand in an irregular manner to mark out the edges of each planting.

When dividing existing plants, use only the vigorous outer portions. The hard and woody centres of clumps of perennials rarely break into growth evenly and produce satisfactory results.

Firm planting is vital, especially on soil that has been recently cultivated. After frosty weather check recent plantings as sometimes they are lifted by severe weather. Once the soil has thawed, gently replant them.

During the spring, liberal quantities of slug pellets should be scattered amongst plants such as lupins, delphiniums and others which produce succulent spring shoots. A ring of ash or weathered soot around each group of vulnerable plants is also a good slug deterent.

A spring mulch with well rotted manure or garden compost is invaluable. Not only does this conserve moisture during warm dry summer weather, but it suppresses seedling weeds too. This applies to established borders as much as to those that are being newly planted.

Herbaceous plants benefit from regular feeding, the most usual method being the liberal application of fertiliser around emerging plants in early spring. Providing that this is done during a wet spell, and the rate recommended for the vegetable plot is not exceeded, then there is unlikely to be any scorching of the foliage.

As soon as vigorous growth starts to be produced, stake those plants that are going to require support. It is infinitely preferable to insert the stakes before the plants start flopping over. A collapsed plant can never be staked tidily.

Annuals

The opportunities for the exploitation of hardy annuals are legion. Their success though, depends upon a bright sunny position, good soil conditions, and most important of all, thinning at the correct time. More leggy and weedy plants result from lack of courage at the thinning stage than any other cultural malady.

Few annual flowers enjoy being transplanted and so are best sown in situ. The soil must be in a good friable condition.

If it is wet and sticky, then delay sowing. Use soil conditions as a guide to seed sowing rather than the calendar.

Always sow the seeds in straight lines, even when filling an irregular patch. The plants soon grow together and disguise this formality and the benefit of being able to clearly identify the seedlings from emerging weeds in invaluable.

As soon as the seedlings are large enough to handle, thin them to the desired spacing. At this stage it is important to add any supports that are needed. Pushing stakes or brushwood amongst sagging plants is unsatisfactory.

Both annual and herbaceous plants need regular manicuring if they are to be kept tidy. As blossoms fade, remove them with the flower stem down to a leaf joint. Do not allow spiky stalks to remain. In many cases the prompt removal of spent flowers will ensure a second crop of blooms.

Spray all plants that are susceptible to mildew with a systemic fungicide. This should be part of a routine which takes place every three weeks or so during the growing period. If you are uncertain which plants are likely to be most susceptible, spray them all, it will do no harm and will ensure protection.

1 Dividing
When dividing existing plants, use only the vigorous outer portions.

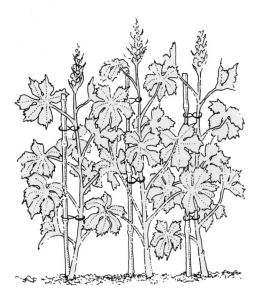

2 Staking
Stake plants as soon as vigorous growth starts to be produced.

Summer bedding selection

The choice of summer bedding plants has never been wider. While traditional gardeners still go for red salvias, blue lobelia and white alyssum, the modern gardener looks to petunias, flowering tobacco and impatiens, all plants that until recent years were of doubtful merit, but with modern varieties are now the backbone of the flower garden.

Traditional bedding

For many years home gardeners looked to the local parks department for inspiration for bedding schemes. Sadly, much of this activity is now in decline and so innovation is not as common as it once was. However, the parks have left domestic gardeners with a great legacy of ideas and plants, many of which still rest easy in our gardens, especially those associated with houses built before 1960.

At this time geraniums were all the rage. They still are, but the modern seed raised bedding geranium is a very different plant from the older bedding type which is annually raised from cuttings and still quite common in the north. Look out for varieties like the single flowered red Paul Crampel, the double red Gustav Emrich and the variegated leafed Happy Thought. Then there are the smaller bedding sorts such as the charming pink flowered Kliene Liebling and the golden variegated Golden Harry Hieover. All these are raised from August cuttings, overwintered and then planted during late spring.

Salvias are very traditional, the bright red Blaze of Fire having been the mainstay of British bedding for years. This is now surpassed by modern varieties like Rodeo and Volcano. The same has not happened with lobelia. For decades the light blue Cambridge Blue and dark blue Crystal Palace have led the way and they continue to do so. The main advance has been the introduction of a stable white variety called White Lady. This should become the replacement in formal bedding schemes for the white alyssum which is not of such neat and refined habit as the lobelias.

White alyssum is still useful for the summer garden, along with its violet-purple companion Violet Queen. So too are the lavateras, especially Silver Cup and Mont

Blanc, pink and white varieties respectively. These are so much more reliable than the traditional lanky pink flowered Loveliness.

Modern bedding

The modern bedding scheme still consists of traditional plants, but in very modern varieties. Petunias which used to be a hit and miss affair are now very much more reliable. Choose the new Resisto strains and they will do well under most conditions in our northern climate. Rarely do the flowers ball-up at the first shower of rain and their length of flowering season is something not dreamt of even ten years ago.

New marigolds are introduced with great regularity. While it is true that many of these varieties have fewer merits than their parents, there have been a number of definite steps forward. Apart from the traditional French and African marigolds we now have Afro-French varieties, but amongst the most exciting recent developments have been the large flowered Inca strains.

Busy lizzies or impatiens are available in almost every size, shape and colour and are excellent for almost all situations except baking sun. They will do well in shade and are excellent subjects for tubs and planters. For reliability choose the Imp strain.

Flowering tobaccos have also made an impact recently. No longer do we have to endure the tall, unstable kinds of yesteryear. Nowadays there are dwarf compact kinds like the incomparable mixed Idol strain.

Down-to-earth tip

When choosing bedding plants always look on the seed packet or plant label for the Fleuroselect logo. This indicates that a variety has an award from that impartial European seed organisation.

This guarantees not only a high quality, free-flowering variety, but one that is tolerant of a wide range of weather conditions, having been successfully trialled as far north as Finland and as far south as Italy.

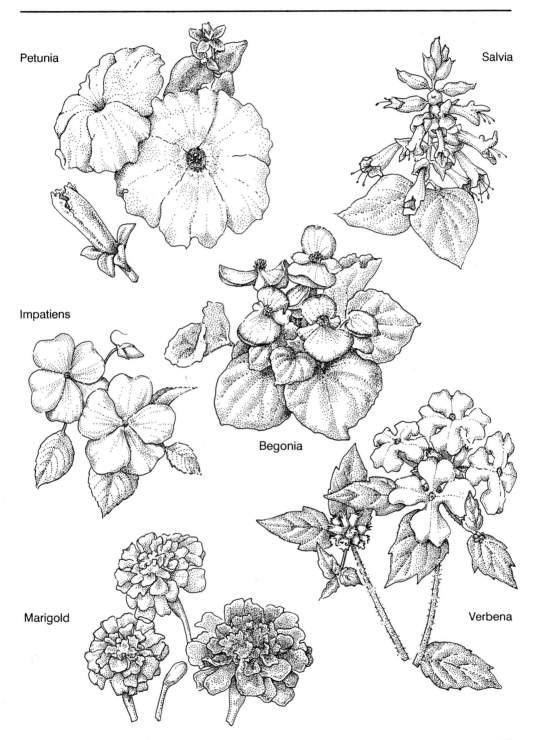

Petunia

Salvia

Impatiens

Begonia

Marigold

Verbena

Raising plants

Although a few summer bedding subjects like pansies can be raised from seed sown directly outside in a garden frame, the majority of popular varieties must be started on a window ledge or in a greenhouse.

Choosing compost

When raising bedding plants from seed indoors, always use trays or pans of a good seed compost. Never be tempted to go out into the garden and scoop up ordinary soil for seed raising.

Unless your garden soil is exceptional, its physical structure will be poor compared with seed compost and not conducive to the successful raising of fine seeded varieties. It is also likely to be host to all manner of pathogens which will cause problems later on.

Purchased seed has the sole object of springing to life, so give it the best chance possible. Seedlings reflect the quality of the compost in which they are growing, so the kind of compost is very important. Unlike potting composts, seed composts have few nutrients in them. These are ideal for seed germination and emergence.

The lack of nutrients is deliberate and ensures that there is unlikely to be damage to tender seedlings and that the growth of moss and liverworts is as far as possible impaired.

Soil based composts, like John Innes Seed Compost, are suitable for all summer bedding plants, but quicker germination and initially better seedlings usually result from soilless mediums.

However, all peat soilless composts should be used with caution. Unless you can be sure of a very smooth surface once the seed tray is filled, it is unwise to sow very fine seeded varieties, for the medium is fibrous and full of air pockets in which tiny seeds can become lost.

All peat composts are best for larger seeded kinds like marigolds. Fine seeded flowers, such as lobelia and petunia can be grown in a soilless compost, but preferably only those that contain a quantity of high quality sand in the mixture.

In any event, whatever is finally decided, always purchase a good branded compost. It is rarely worth considering mixing your own. The resulting medium can be very variable and the young plants unpredictable.

As germination takes place it is wise to water freshly emerged seedlings with Cheshunt Compound. This is a fungicide which prevents the occurrence of damping off disease, an easily recognised disorder which causes seedlings to collapse. The base of their stems turns brown and rots.

Pricking out

Once the seedlings have germinated they can be pricked out. They should ideally have their seed or cotyledon leaves fully expanded and the first true leaf showing before transplanting. Care must be taken with handling as they are very delicate and often brittle. Never hold a seedling by its root or stem, always by the tip of a seed leaf.

Individual seedlings are lifted from the clusters in which they germinated and spaced out into a pan or seed tray. Standard seed trays will comfortably accommodate 35 plants, although with smaller growing varieties as many as 45 seedlings can be grown.

It is usual to prick out seedlings slightly lower in the compost than in the tray or pan in which they germinated, in most cases burying the stem up to the level of the seed leaves. This only applies if the seedlings are short, strong and healthy. Burying a lanky seedling will result in its collapse.

It is usual to prick seedlings out into potting compost rather than seed compost as they are going to require considerable nourishment. Any standard soilless potting compost should serve, although feeding with a liquid manure may be necessary later on.

John Innes Compost No. 1 is the most satisfactory soil-based compost to use, although this will also need regular feeding a month or so before the plants are put out in the garden.

Providing that there are not severe temperature fluctuations and always plenty of light, the plants should grow on well. Apart from perhaps mildew and greenfly, few problems are likely to be encountered. Both of these can be easily countered with any of the popular systemic fungicides or insecticides currently available.

Hardening off

The most critical time in the raising of half-hardy subjects is the weaning period – that period when the plants are eased out of their comfortable greenhouse or kitchen windowsill atmosphere prior to planting in the open garden.

A cold frame is invaluable for weaning, for in cold weather the frame top can remain in place, whereas if the weather turns warmer it can be removed entirely. What must be achieved is a gradual tolerance of lower temperatures over a period of two or three weeks without giving the plants a check.

First of all the frame top is lifted to permit ventilation. This is gradually increased until it can be removed entirely during the day time. It can then be raised at night to allow ventilation, excpet when a frost threatens. Eventually the top can be removed both day and night unless a chill wind or heavy rain is forecast.

If the spring is long and cold and the roots of the plants fill the seed trays completely, a weak liquid feed will help to keep them in good condition without promoting unnatural growth.

Using plugs

A recent phenomenon with summer bedding plants has been the introduction of the plug. This is a very narrow plug of compost which fits into a modular tray.

Commercially large numbers of plugs are produced on what amounts to a factory farming system whereby production is computer controlled and individual seeds are sown in plugs and yield as near perfect plants as possible.

Until recently plugs were produced by specialists for commerical bedding plant growers, the young plantlets being grown on and then sold to amateur gardeners.

Now it is possible in many garden centres to find plugs of a wide range of bedding subjects available directly to home gardeners. These have the advantage of being all at the correct shape of growth, all of even stature and at a time in their life when, providing they are well watered and kept frost-free, they are likely to succeed.

Before planting plugs into pots or seed trays, be sure that the core of compost is very damp. If this has dried out and is then placed in damp compost it is likely to become isolated and suffer a set-back. Stand dry plugs in a tray of water until thoroughly damp.

Plugs may seem an easy way of producing bedding plants, but they are restrictive in so for as there are only a limited number of varieties offered like this at the moment. However, if the varieties that you want are available, then it is a very cost effective way of obtaining high quality plants.

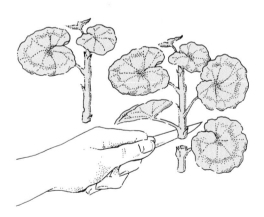

Softwood cuttings

Another way to increase summer bedding plant stock is to take cuttings. To take softwood cuttings from plants such as geranium slice a 3in long tip of young growth just below a leaf joint or node and remove the lower leaves. Soak in fungicide then insert in compost.

Containers, planters ...

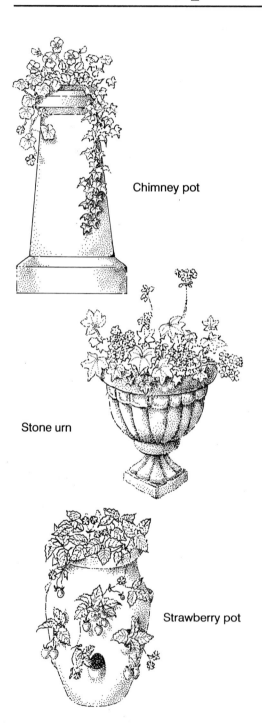

Chimney pot

Stone urn

Strawberry pot

Growing plants in containers and window boxes is becoming increasingly popular. Modern materials have made production of all kinds of tubs, planters and window boxes more economical than ever before. In addition, scientifically formulated no-soil composts can virtually guarantee success. There is no longer any need to have large bulky urns and troughs that take two people to move, nor to struggle with a soil that is of inadequate structure.

For the gardener with only a small backyard, planters and window boxes offer the only real opportunity for introducing colour and interest. The mobility of tubs and planters is also a great virtue. If a particular arrangement is not pleasing it can easily be changed. Fair weather gardeners can decide only to garden during the summer and abandon the planters to the garage or potting shed for the winter. Winter gardening need consist of no more than sweeping the patio or yard.

For the enthusiast a container or window box provides a great opportunity for making an intensive floral picture. The gardener is pitting his wits against nature and yet it almost always comes off. This pushing of plants to their limits and succeeding is largely the result of the development of modern composts. Within the confines of a container nowadays it is possible to create colour of a richness, diversity and intensity not possible elsewhere in the garden. Plants can be packed closely together and providing they are watched for diseases and carefully manicured, they will prosper.

While this intensity of cultivation and spectacle of colour appeals to both the keen gardener and the householder with little but hard landscaping, it is also very welcome for those who find it increasingly difficult to bend. Carefully selected containers and window boxes can be cultivated at a reasonable height. For the elderly or infirm gardener, containers and window boxes are the perfect answer.

Choosing a container

Any container, planter or window box must have a minimum depth of 6 in. if it is to allow for proper root development. Indeed, a greater depth is more desirable. Bearing

... and window boxes

this in mind, carefully assess any urn or similar container with a shallow area around the rim before purchase. If the outer planting is unable to penetrate the main central body of compost then with constant drying out the plants will be permanently stressed.

Drainage must also be provided, preferably by holes in the base of the planter or window box, although in containers without holes a generous layer of gravel in the bottom before soil or compost is added will often work with careful watering.

Containers that are to be used all year round must also be frost-proof. Not only the materials from which they are made, but also to some extent the insulation that they can provide for the roots of plants. Thin-walled plastic tubs are light and easy to handle but permit easy passage of cold while wooden tubs, although heavy and unwieldy, provide considerable insulation.

Along with drainage, resistance to extremes of temperature is vital for the success of year-round plantings. Plants that are normally hardy in the open ground often succumb to root kill in a container which freezes solid during the winter. This also indicates that it is important to have as large a container as possible for any plantings that are to remain outside all winter. The greater the volume of compost the less likely freezing is to be a problem.

The weight of a container can also be an important consideration. If a planting is going to be tall, such as might be the case with a shrub, then the container should be large enough that when filled with compost it is stable. Leafy half-standard box or bay trees can easily be tipped over in the wind if growing in a less than substantial planter.

On the other hand, a lightweight material is desirable for window boxes or any other types of planters that are fixed to a wall. The lighter the material, the more weighty, substantial and generally better the compost can be.

Selecting plants

Fortunately, most of our summer flowering annuals and bedding plants are easy going and co-exist quite happily with one another. However, to create the best quality display in a container or window box a single plant type should be grown. This means that the compost can be prepared for that plant's specific requirement and the subsequent watering and maintenance regime tailored exactly to its needs.

Geraniums for example enjoy full, uninterrupted sunshine in a free-draining compost which is not too rich. If there is a high level of plant foods, especially nitrogen, then the plants will produce foliage at the expense of flowers. A lean hungry compost in a hot location will ensure a colourful summer-long spectacle.

Busy lizzies or impatiens on the other hand prefer a partially shaded location and a compost that has a high proportion of organic matter. Recent research has indicated that busy lizzies prefer a compost containing a composted pulverised bark, a constituent which geraniums would dislike. So one can readily appreciate that a container in which geraniums and impatiens are mixed is only going to meet with moderate success.

Tuberous rooted begonias will make a cheerful, long lasting summer display for window box or planter. Both the upright growing and pendulous varieties can be grown, but the large flowered sorts are not really suitable. Choose regular commercial strains which are usually sold by colour.

Fibrous rooted begonias are another good choice, but do not mix these with double flowered tuberous kinds. These are the small flowered begonias that flower from early summer into the autumn, only succumbing to the first sharp frost. They are available in colours that range from white through various pinks to deep red.

Bulbous plants are amongst the most versatile for container cultivation. Indeed, such is their diversity that it is possible to find a variety to suit almost every situation imaginable. Whether as feature plants themselves or complimentary highlights they provide reliable colour.

There are many gems amongst the summer flowering bulbs, especially the lilies, but tiger flowers, sparaxis and African corn lilies can make a bold showing. Of course the use of containers in spring is to be highly commended and this is where bulbs of all kinds really come into their own.

Hanging baskets

Hanging baskets are amongst the most traditional of gardening features. They provide highlights for a conventional setting and yet with a small backyard are often the garden itself. Adaptable and colourful they add interest to the most mundane surroundings very cheaply and easily.

Preparing the basket

The successful aftercare of a hanging basket depends as much upon its preparation as any other factor. The type of compost used is very important, the modern soilless brands being well balanced to ensure even growth and light in weight to enable the basket to be suspended almost anywhere safely. As it is always difficult to maintain moisture because of the constant drying effects of the wind, it is useful to add a little perlite to the compost before planting. This is a white granular material derived from a volcanic rock which is capable of absorbing moisture and allowing it to be released back into the compost in drier periods. Up to a quarter by volume of perlite can be added to good effect.

Although there are now many different kinds of hanging pots and baskets available to the home gardener, the traditional wire basket with its lining of green sphagnum moss is still the most popular and visually appealing. They are not as difficult to establish as you might at first imagine, for the moss is built up gradually and systematically layer by layer.

Trailing plants are pushed through the sides of the basket, the roots making firm

---

Down-to-earth tip

Sometimes a hanging basket will dry out. Providing that the plants have only wilted and the leaves are not shrivelled, it will not be beyond redemption. Soilless compost consists largely of peat and once dry is often difficult to wet again. The water runs around in globules on the surface of the compost and will not penetrate it properly. If a small quantity of dishwashing liquid is added to the water it will soak through as if by magic. This only works with soilless composts, not the soil based kinds.

---

contact with the compost and the moss tucked neatly around them. The building of the basket continues on upwards.

When filled with compost, remove the pot from the plant that is to form the centrepiece. Place this pot in the centre of the basket and plant around it then remove the pot and drop the pot ball of the centre-piece into the waiting hole. This makes filling the basket simple and ensures even plant distribution around the perimeter.

A newly planted basket must be very carefully watered. If a watering can is used the water may often flow irregularly through the open-sided basket. It is always better to soak them in a deep bowl until the compost has settled, taking care to avoid damaging any trailing shoots. A watering can may be used subsequently providing that a fine rose attachment is used.

The correct watering of hanging baskets is as important as the correct compost. It is vital that they are thoroughly soaked regularly rather than constantly sprinkled with water. If good drainage has been provided surplus water will quickly run away.

Choosing plants

The range of plants available now for growing in hanging baskets is greater than ever before. Plant plug production, the modern and very economical method of raising bedding and basket plants in tiny compost modules, has revolutionised the range of plants available as growers have searched for new varieties which adapt to this intensive method of culture.

Traditional hanging baskets are still planted with combinations of pendulous fuchsias, ivy leafed geraniums, trailing lobelia, dwarf French marigolds and petunias. There is nothing at all wrong with this, for long-lasting and reliable colour is assured in a basket that is well clothed with foliage. When carefully considered though, it is quite remarkable that geraniums and fuchsias flourish together, for each has a very different range of cultural needs. When grown together the result is a compromise.

So perhaps the modern gardener should look a little more carefully at the actual requirements of individual plants and consider single plant variety baskets. Geraniums, fuchsias and impatiens are all suitable plants for such mono-culture. Not only do they have specialised compost requirements, but each grows better in a different location. A basket of ivy-leafed geraniums will enjoy a hot sunny corner in a free draining gritty compost, while impatiens would grow better in a compost with plenty of pulverised bark added in a shadowy spot.

Themed baskets

Single plant hanging baskets provide great opportunities for colour theming. For some years it has been fashionable for gardeners to produce blue, white or pink borders, but it is only very recently that themed baskets have been introduced. Modern strains of geraniums like Mini-Cascade are perfect for such plantings, making huge balls of bright colour. If single colour fuchsia varieties are chosen an equally lovely effect can be achieved. The elegant Red Spider and pure white Annabel are two hanging varieties that always grow well.

Pendulous begonias can be used in a similar way. It is amongst these easily grown tuberous-rooted plants that the greatest range of colourful basket plants can be found. From pure white, through yellow and pink to deep fiery red. There are one or two named varieties around, but the majority are sold by colour. For an intensely colourful show pendulous begonias can be depended upon.

Hanging carnations are also reliable. Colourful and often richly fragrant, they require a very free-draining compost. However, they do not like to dry out and so very careful placing is necessary. Known as Tyrolean carnations they are also useful in window boxes, bringing a hint of the Austrian Tyrol.

Despite the obvious benefits of single plant variety hanging baskets, mixed plantings should not be neglected. For informal gardens they are essential. While traditional mixtures of geraniums, fuchsias and lobelia are still very popular, the adventurous gardener should be on the lookout for some of the more unusual varieties on offer. Apart from the lovely blue brachycombe, recent introductions have included the yellow flowered bidens, variegated felicia or kingfisher daisy, the bright blue lobelia – like scaevola, all beautiful plants that thoroughly enjoy life in a basket.

1 Perimeter planting

Fill basket with compost, place pot from centre-piece specimen then plant round it.

2 Centre planting

Remove pot and put centre plant into the waiting hole.

Chrysanthemums, dahlias, roses

There are some plants that gardeners take to their hearts and which become an obsession. These are all very popular subjects for garden decoration and cutting which should be found in every ornamental garden.

Chrysanthemums

All the popular chrysanthemum varieties are increased from cuttings. These arise from overwintered rootstocks or stools which have been placed in boxes of damp compost and stood in a warm light place.

Cuttings should be taken when 1 in. long, removed at a leaf joint and placed in an equal parts by volume mixture of peat and sharp sand or peat and perlite under glass. Once rooted the cuttings must be potted immediately and gradually weaned to cooler temperatures before being planted out towards the end of May.

It is wise to provide each plant with a stake at planting time. If the plants have not sent out side-shoots of their own accord by mid-June the growing points should be re-moved to make the plants break.

The resulting side shoots may grow on satisfactorily, but if they try to produce a flower bud too soon they should also have their growing points removed. As the plants grow they must be regularly tied in and as flower buds develop the strongest should be retained and the clusters of smaller buds around it removed. Earwigs make themselves a nuisance and should be controlled by dusting around the plants with an insecticidal dust. Greenfly and other insect pests can be warded off by regularly spraying with a systemic insecticide. When autumn comes and the first frosts blacken the plants they should be cut back almost to the ground, lifted and placed in deep trays of dryish peat or soil and stored in a light frost-free place.

Dahlias

Dahlias are raised initially rather like chrysanthemums, short cuttings being rooted from shoots that arise during spring from

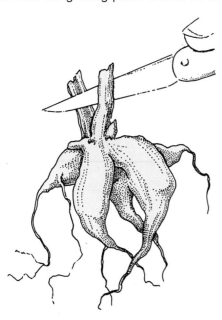

1 Tuber division

Divide the swollen roots into portions, each with at least one crown bud.

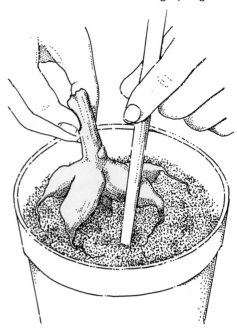

2 Tuber potting

Pot the cuttings when the cut surfaces have formed a corky layer.

... and sweet peas

boxed tubers. Pot freshly rooted plants immediately and slowly harden them off.

Although it is not essential, it is helpful to stake dahlias as you plant them. Obviously they will not need tying in initially, but the early placement of stakes prevents damaging the root system. Supplied with plenty of water and regularly tied in to ensure support, particularly during wet and windy weather, reasonable blossoms will be produced without any trouble. Dahlia growers who want flowers for showing or cutting disbud the flowering heads when embryo buds have formed. This entails retaining the strongest bud on a single stem and rubbing out subsidiary and lateral buds.

Dahlias will continue flowering until the first sharp frost. This blackens the foliage and signals the time for lifting. Before making a start take a close look at the main stem. If it seems succulent and green, leave the plants to endure a further frost. The blackening of the stems by frost is the finest way to seal the wound where foliage becomes detached from the tuber.

Tubers that have been properly frosted are lifted as soon as possible and spread out under cover to dry. This enables surplus soil to be shaken off when dry. Tubers should be inverted to allow surplus water in the cut stems to drain away. When prepared for storage they can be placed in trays or dry peat or sawdust and kept in a frost-free place until returned to deep boxes for cutting production during February and March. Before storing it is useful to dust the tubers with sulphur to deter storage moulds.

Roses

Roses are amongst the most popular garden flowers. There are bush or tea varieties as well as floribundas, climbers, ramblers, miniatures and old fashioned shrub roses.

Amongst popular varieties that always do well in the north are the lovely pink Blessings, Benson and Hedges Gold, Whisky Mac and the bright red National Trust. Floribundas that consistently perform well are the pink Queen Elizabeth, bright red Lili Marlene, Iceberg and the low-growing orange-flowered Anna Ford. Of the climbing sorts, the pink Compassion is superb, while amongst the miniatures the multi-coloured

Baby Masquerade always does well.

Roses can be planted bare rooted at any time during their dormant period. Providing that all the leaves have fallen it is safe to plant them, although container grown roses can obviously be planted all the year round.

Good soil preparation is vital for successful roses. Plenty of well rotted compost incorporated into the soil together with a liberal dusting of bonemeal will ensure a quick get-away in the spring.

Roses are grafted onto a rootstock. You can quite clearly see the union. When planting ensure that this union is just above soil level. Reduce the height of the bushes at planting time by about one third to prevent them blowing about. Final pruning should be left until the spring when they should be cut back to two or three buds.

Sweet peas

Sweet peas can be sown either during the autumn or the spring. Sow two seeds to a pot and when they germinate thin out to a single seedling.

Sweet pea plants that have been properly grown and acclimatised in a frame are quite hardy and can be planted out at the end of March or early April.

To grow really good sweet peas it is essential that the soil is properly prepared. Liberal quantities of well rotted manure or garden compost should have been dug in during the winter. This not only provides a little nourishment, but conserves vital moisture during the summer.

Bud and flower drop later on can usually be associated with a variable soil moisture content. Plenty of organic matter in the soil helps to maintain moisture consistently.

There are several methods of growing sweet peas but where twiggy material is available then rounded clumps some 6 ft high placed at intervals in the border is the most satisfactory method of combining garden decoration with a source of cut flowers. Pea and bean netting can also be used if well supported.

Routine summer cultivation involves the removal of faded blossoms and their stalks to encourage a longer flowering season, regular watering in dry spells and an occasional feed with a liquid manure.

Spring bedding plants

Spring flowering bedding plants differ from their summer flowering counterparts in that they are predominantly hardy, can be raised easily from seed sown in the open ground, and are mostly biennials.

This means that they have two cycles of growth. The first produces foliage and a healthy plant able to survive the winter, the second leads to flowering, thus the plant effectively lives for two years. In the garden the effect is the same, but for economy of space, and by carefully timing sowings, the plants can be persuaded to complete the growth cycles in scarcely more than one.

A few subjects are perennials, although only short-lived unless lifted and divided regularly. These include polyanthus and primrose. Other perennial subjects, such as wallflowers, deteriorate after their first flush of youth and are best replaced each year.

Bulbs always figure prominently in a spring bedding display and an awareness of their value when associated with spring bedding subjects is essential if you are to make the most of your spring display.

Planning a display

Have a design in mind for spring bedding before sowing any seeds. This ensures you have all the plants to hand when the summer display is removed and saves production of additional unwanted material. It also enables you to grow precisely the numbers you want and in varieties that are going to complete flowering by the time they are replaced with summer bedding.

Summer bedding plants have to be planted out during late May or early June so it is vital that the spring bedding display is cleared by then. It is therefore important that the flowering periods of each subject in the display coincide, and are past their best before they have to be removed. This rarely arises at the other end of the season as frost has usually finished the summer display in time.

Raising Spring bedding plants

There are two methods of raising spring flowering bedding plants. Wallflowers, for example are easiest raised in the open ground, while forget-me-not, pansies, polyanthus and double daisies are best grown in trays or pots. All should be sown

between the end of May and mid-July in order to produce plants that will withstand the winter.

Those best raised in the open garden should be sown in shallow drills made with the edge of a swan-neck hoe in a nursery bed, which could well be a corner of the vegetable plot. If this is what you intend, include wallflowers in the section reserved for cabbages, cauliflowers and sprouts. Like brassicas, wallflowers are subject to devastating attacks from club root disease.

Before sowing, water the open drills and ensure that the soil is thoroughly moistened. The seed can then be distributed thinly along the bottom of the drill and back filled, ensuring that if the weather remains dry, the drill receives another soaking.

Seedlings of wallflowers appear within a few days and so it is as well to be ready to dust them with an insecticidal dust as a precaution against flea beetle.

When the first few adult leaves appear, the vigorous young seedlings should be transplanted into nursery rows about three or four inches apart with ten inches between the rows. As soon as these transplants have become established, the growing points should be pinched out so that they bush out and become more substantial plants.

Planting out

Open ground plants can be moved to their final positions any time after the summer bedding has been cleared away. It is difficult to establish spring flowering bedding subjects after the end of October, so if the season lingers the summer bedding must be removed and the soil prepared before then. Adequate soil preparation is vital, although fresh manure is not desirable. A slow release fertiliser like bonemeal applied before planting, together with very firm planting, will ensure the success of most spring flowering subjects. During the winter frost may lift the plants. After severe weather always check to make sure that their roots are not exposed. Remove any faded foliage during the winter as this provides a haven for slugs which can be a major spring pest. As a precaution it is useful to scatter slug bait amongst the plants once severe winter weather is over.

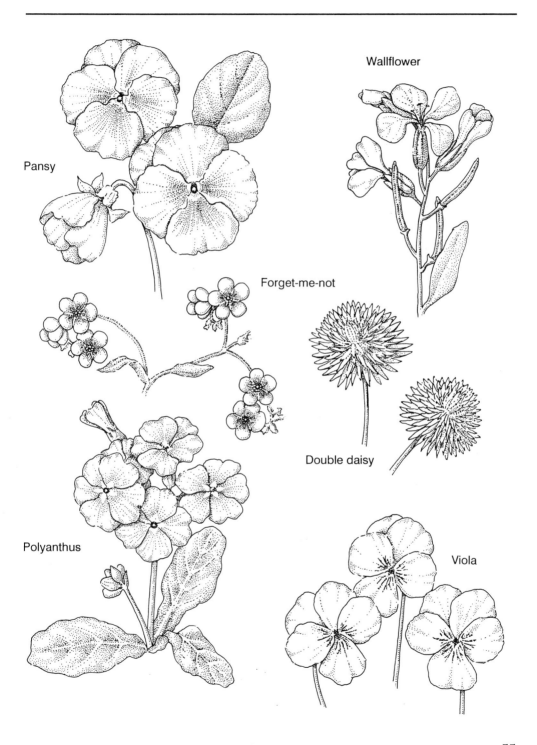

Pansy

Wallflower

Forget-me-not

Double daisy

Polyanthus

Viola

Spring flowering bulbs

Daffodils

Daffodils and tulips are amongst the most popular spring flowering bulbs, both being available in a diversity of shapes, size, colour and form that offer something for everyone. Daffodils are botanically Narcissus, although to gardeners daffodils are those which have large trumpets, while narcissus are the small cupped varieties.

Newcomers to gardening will probably be tempted to select old well tried kinds like Carlton, Golden Harvest and King Alfred. Dependable though these may be, they have nowadays been surpassed by modern free-flowering sorts such as Spellbinder, Rembrandt and the appropriately named Unsurpassable. All are a rich golden yellow, except for Spellbinder which is an irridescent sulphurous shade.

Not all daffodils are yellow though, Ice Follies being a cool icy white, while Mrs R.O. Backhouse is shell pink. Some are fully double, like the aged but invaluable Texas and equally endearing Inglescombe. The small cupped kinds that gardeners loosely refer to as narcissus are typified by Geranium and Actaea. Both have broad flat white petals and orange or red cups.

Tulips

Tulips offer us equal diversity, with some varieties flowering as early as March and others as late as the end of May. Like narcissus, tulips fall into clearly defined groups, which, although having no botanical significance, are widely accepted by gardeners to identify different kinds.

Single early tulips are short growing kinds, typified by Kreizerskroon, the red and gold tulip popular with public conservatories. While many of the recent introductions within this group can be used for pot culture, they grow just as well outdoors.

Flowering during April, they are more commonly used in formal planting schemes although there is no reason why they should not provide colourful spring highlights in the informal garden.

Darwin tulips are later flowering and are those which are popularly used for spring bedding with a carpet of forget-me-nots. Rose Copeland has lovely blossoms of carmine and silvery rose, while Princess

Elizabeth is pink and William Pitt a vivid scarlet.

It is from the union of these two groups that the triumph tulips have been derived. Similar in many ways to Darwin, they flower much earlier and are of shorter habit.

The species tulips and their hybrids make excellent subjects for informal gardens, especially those that are exposed and windy. Not only are they tough and resilient, but of a much neater habit.

Miscellaneous bulbs

Look in any bulb catalogue and behind the hyacinths, tulips and narcissus will be a section entitled Miscellaneous Bulbs, a mixture of mostly short growing characters of infinite beauty and diversity. These range from the snakeshead fritillary and dwarf iris, to snowdrops, aconites and scillas.

There are many different kinds of scillas, but none more lovely than Tubergen's squill. A pale blue gem that flowers from late February throughout March with delicate blossoms that are striped with dark blue. An excellent plant for pan culture in the alpine house, this is equally at home outdoors, tolerating the most hostile spring weather. When planted beneath shrubs it forms a dense carpet.

The Siberian squill is equally prolific, but flowers a trifle later with more pendant blossoms of intense Prussian-blue. This is excellent for naturalising. It seeds itself freely and quickly forms sizeable colonies.

Snowdrops are available in a number of varieties. Apart from the common much loved species there is the double flowered form and one known as the donkey-eared snowdrop on account of its upright green sepals. These all flower from January onwards.

Winter aconites blossom at the same time, producing a carpet of yellow beneath trees and shrubs. The leaf canopy does not permit anything to grow here during summer. In winter the trees are dormant and the aconites can hold sway, transforming a problem area into a picture of great beauty for three weeks of the year.

Chionodoxa, or glory of the snow, has bright blue blossoms with distinct white eyes which are often to be seen pushing through the snow during early spring. This is a self-seeding bulb that rapidly makes dense carpets beneath trees and shrubs in the same way as winter aconites.

The dwarf iris species are excellent for the rock garden, especially the popular blue reticulate iris. This is available in a range of shades and in named varieties. Choose the cobalt blue Cantab and deep velvety blue Harmony or Natasha, the first true white.

Selecting bulbs

Whenever possible select your own bulbs, discarding anything that is soft or discoloured. With narcissus, feel the base plate from where the roots will emanate, and if it feels soft then pass it over. Similarly avoid crocus or tulips that have lost their tunics. The skins on bulbs provide protection, and when planted without it they are vulnerable to all kinds of diseases and disorders.

Snowdrops should be carefully inspected for signs of grey mould and the tiny bulbous iris must have clean, whitish skins. When black patches are in evidence, avoid the bulbs for they are suffering from the contagious ink spot disease.

Larger bulbs always yield the best results, so go for the biggest that you can afford. Multi-nosed narcissus are an excellent buy and if you want a breathtaking display of hyacinths purchase the largest size.

Propagating bulbs

Some spring flowering bulbs, such as daffodils, reproduce themselves from division quite naturally. The individual bulb increases in size and eventually divides producing daughter bulbs. If left to their own devices these eventually separate completely and form part of an ever-increasing clump. To hasten this process and give new young bulbs the best opportunity of developing rapidly, established groups of daffodils can be lifted every four or five years and all the daughter bulbs can be separated out. It is important when removing such bulbs that each has at least a vestige of base plate from which new roots can be produced, or they will not survive.

Tulips are altogether different. They are reproduced annually and so need looking after very carefully after flowering. The per-

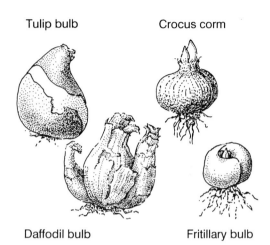

Tulip bulb   Crocus corm

Daffodil bulb   Fritillary bulb

formance of the foliage is crucial to their well being as it is this which builds up the new bulbs and determines whether or not they will attain flowering size. Tulips generally yield several bulbs from one individual quite naturally. Their success is dependant upon the bulbs remaining undisturbed and being regularly fed from flower bud break until the foliage first starts to fade.

Hyacinths can be assisted by the gardener. These will reproduce slowly by themselves, but masses of new bulbs can be produced by a process known as scooping or scoring. Scooping is usually only undertaken by commercial growers as there is little leeway for error. Scoring is much simpler but effective, although not as many young bulbs are produced from each adult.

The principle behind both methods is interference with the base plate and through this the encouragement of spawning or bulbil production. Scooping involves removing all except the outer rim of the base plate, whereas scoring is the removal of slivers of tissue across the base plate to form a cross. The bulbs are planted as normal after this operation. They grow well, but in addition to producing leaves and flowers they also yield masses of tiny bulbs around the scooped or cut areas. These can be removed and grown on as individuals.

Summer flowering bulbs

Spring is traditionally thought of as bulb time but there is a very interesting range of colourful characters available for summer flowering. A few are permanent inhabitants of the garden, but the majority are treated like bedding plants and removed in winter.

Gladioli

Gladioli are amongst the loveliest summer flowering bulbs, producing bold brightly coloured spikes of blossom through August and September. The large flowered hybrids are perfect for cutting while the dwarfer kinds are also suitable for general border decoration. Gladioli corms or bulbs can be planted where they are to flower. In an informal setting they can be planted in clumps at random, but where they are being grown for cutting it is much more convenient to arrange them in rows.

Cover the corms by about their own depth of soil and as soon as young shoots emerge carefully place a strong cane beside each. As leafy growth develops tie them in to their supports. Providing they are kept weed-free, gladioli are easily grown, especially if planted in a warm, sunny sheltered position.

After flowering, the plants should be encouraged to continue growing until frost blackens the foliage. The corms can then be lifted and dried off in a cool airy place. When the corms have dried out all the remaining soil can be gently rubbed off and the decaying foliage removed.

Dusting with flowers of sulphur is a useful precaution against storage moulds before the corms are suspended in nets in a frost-free place. Regular inspection for signs of decay should be made during the winter and any doubtful corms must be removed. However, most will remain sound and healthy for spring planting.

Lilies

Lilies are highlights of the summer flower garden. Brightly coloured and with exotic blossoms, they are frequently regarded as difficult to grow. While there are one or two temperamental kinds, those that are popularly available are reliable if provided with suitable growing conditions. The majority of lilies prefer a free draining soil of acid persuasion, and on heavy clay soils benefit from a generous quantity of sharp sand or grit incorporated into the soil before planting. It is also prudent to sprinkle a little sand into the bottom of each planting hole for the bulbs to rest on. This assists drainge and also encourages rapid root development.

If your soil is not in good physical condition it is better to start the bulbs off in a soil-less potting compost or peat, moving them to permanent positions when they are actively growing and outdoor conditions are more favourable.

The majority of lilies have strong, vigorous shoots which turn into sturdy flowering stems that rarely require staking. When a large flowered variety is being grown and a cane is necessary for support, try to arrange to insert this at planting time to avoid damaging the bulb on its roots.

In general, lilies are easy plants to grow. They suffer from few pests and diseases, especially when growing in a well managed garden. The Mid-Century hybrids are amongst the best varieties, although tiger and martagon lilies are reliable traditional sorts.

Other bulbs

Acidantheras look rather like gladioli, but flower later. These have spires of white blossoms with purple throats and a most delicious heady fragrance. These are like the ordinary gladioli in so far as they require lifting and storing for the winter. So do tiger flowers or tigridias. These add a touch of the tropical to a garden, looking rather like orchids and in an infinite range of colours. Each blossom lasts a single day, but so many are produced that there is a continuous show from July until September.

Florists' anemones will flower for most of the summer too. Grow the De Caen and St. Brigid strains for the maximum effect. Plant the black raisin-like rootstocks from spring through to summer for long-lasting display.

The giant summer hyacinth is also worth growing. Planted during early spring it will produce towering spires of waxy cream bell-like blossoms during late summer. A hardy and permanent bulb.

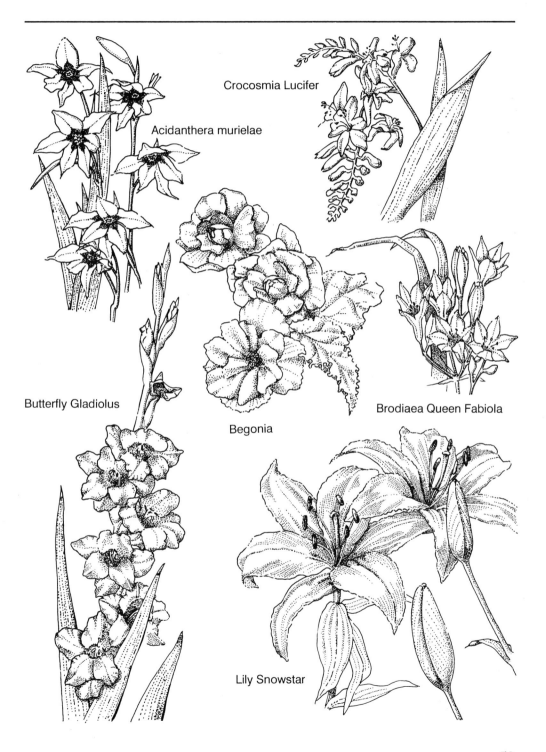

Crocosmia Lucifer

Acidanthera murielae

Butterfly Gladiolus

Begonia

Brodiaea Queen Fabiola

Lily Snowstar

59

Autumn, winter flowering bulbs

Perhaps not thought of as a usual time for bulbs to be flowering, the autumn sees the blossoming of some of our loveliest subjects. There are varieties that can extend the season from September until November. Once December comes, forced bulbs provide colour, but of course these have to be grown indoors. They provide a welcome breath of spring in the dark and dismal depths of winter.

Autumn flowering bulbs

Hardy autumn flowering bulbs have a very short planting season. They become available in shops and garden centres during mid-July and they must be planted by the end of August.

Colchicums are one of the most popular autumn flowering subjects. Some people confuse these with autumn crocus, for they have the appearance of a giant crocus when in flower.

Others call them naked ladies because they produce their handsome lilac, purple or white blossoms before their bulky glossy green foliage appears.

There are numerous kinds from which to choose, with the majority of them flowering during September and early October. The lilac flowered *Colchicum speciosum* is the most widely available, together with its white form *album* and the fully double lilac variety Waterlily.

The true autumn crocus is typified by the meadow saffron, a small flowered species with delicate rosy-purple flowers. *Crocus speciosus* is very similar and has yielded some superb varieties, amongst them the blue Oxonian, pale violet-blue Pollux and the lavender Cassiope. All flower between September and November.

Sternbergia is a similar proposition to the autumn crocus. Becoming increasingly popular, this bright yellow flowered crocus-like plant flowers during September and October. Apart from being a successful garden plant, it is most useful for indoor pot work in an unheated greenhouse.

All the crocus type bulbs should be planted immediately they come to hand, but colchicums can be persuaded to flower without planting. Being sizeable bulbs with a large food reserve, it is common practice to stand them on the window ledge without soil or water and let them blossom. They will not come to any harm providing the bulbs are planted immediately the flowers fade.

The exotic nerine

The hardy nerine is a rather exotic looking bulbous plant which seems incongrous growing outside. Despite its tropical appearance it is perfectly hardy and flowers freely when planted in a situation to its liking. A south or west facing aspect is preferable, the base of a wall being ideal. It likes a good baking from the sun, yet at the same time will not flourish in very dry, impoverished soil.

Delicate rosy-pink flowers are produced on strong stems before there is any significant leaf growth, usually from September through to November. The bulbs sometimes take a short while to settle down before flowering, preferring to grow in crowded conditions where they can stand almost shoulder to shoulder.

Winter bulbs indoors

For a good show of bulbs indoors during the winter early planting is vital. All bulbs must be in by the middle of September, earlier still if the Christmas period is targeted.

Amongst the most successful of all forced bulbs are hyacinths. The first bulbs in the shops are usually prepared to ensure early flowering.

Always purchase the best bulbs that you can afford and use a proper compost or bulb fibre. Specially prepared bulb fibre is generally the best, for it has an open free-draining structure which is a great advantage when shallow bowls are used.

When planting hyacinths in bowls, leave the 'nose' of each bulb just poking out above the surface of the bulb fibre, and always plant a single variety to each bowl, otherwise there will be no uniformity of flowering. Varieties of hyacinth, even of the same colour, can flower as far apart as three or four weeks. Even within a single variety the flower spikes may vary from plant to plant in their period of opening.

If you are growing several bowls of the same variety, then plant all the bulbs together in a deep tray. Once they are well rooted, put those with comparable rates of growth in the same bowl. They will quickly re-establish if lifted carefully with a rootball. This is how the florist achieves even flower spikes and matching heights in a single bowl.

The most important factor in growing successful forcing bulbs, whether they are hyacinths, narcissus or tulips, is the initial rooting period. Once planted, the bulbs must remain in a cool place for between eight and 11 weeks. Tulips must have the longer period.

This enables the bulbs to make a root system that is capable of coping with the burgeoning growth associated with forcing. During their cool period check periodically to see that the bulb fibre remains moist, but never allow it to become wet.

Forcing

After as short a period as eight weeks the flower buds of hyacinths and narcissus will be showing signs of emerging from the bulbs. They can then be moved to light and progressively warmer conditions.

As with most flowering pot plants, forced bulbs must be given maximum light during the short, dull days but must also be given a temperature that is sufficiently low to prevent growth from becoming distorted or elongated.

A window is fine, but do not shut them behind the curtains in the evening as the temperature drop can be sudden and quite damaging. If a suitable light to temperature ratio can be attained the average bowl of hyacinths is good for four or five weeks.

Once flowering has finished, the bulbs are best discarded. Unlike daffodils, which will give a reasonable show the following year when planted out in the garden, hyacinths exhaust themselves when forced and rarely produce more than a few leaves and a sickly flower stalk. The same applies to any tulips that have been grown indoors.

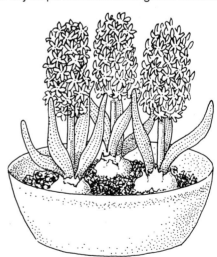

1 Single hyacinths

Plant single hyacinths in pots of bulb fibre or in a special bulb glass full of water. Once planted the bulbs must remain in a cool place for eight to 11 weeks.

2 Bowls of hyacinths

Always plant a single variety of hyacinths to each bowl, or there will be no uniformity of flowering. Varieties even of the same colour can flower as far apart as four weeks.

Wildlife gardening

Wildlife gardening is one of the most popular pursuits, with gardeners not only planting wild flowers but adding garden plants which attract insects, bees and butterflies.

Butterflies

Of all our garden wildlife butterflies are likely to provide the most enjoyment, especially if you plant buddleia. Popularly known as butterfly bushes, they host crowds of peacock and tortoiseshell butterflies on warm days.

The common variety is *Buddleia davidii*, a quck growing medium-sized shrub with green lance-shaped leaves and fragrant pale lilac or purple blossoms carried in graceful arching plumes. Empire Blue is the loveliest variety with a stiff upright habit. White Profusion and White Bouquet are aptly named. For something a little darker try Black Knight or Royal Red.

Autumn flowering *Sedum spectabile* is another wonderful butterfly plant, a hardy dwarf herbaceous perennial with light fleshy foliage and large fluffy heads of deep rose-pink flowers. Varieties Autumn Joy and Meteor are productive and weather resistant.

Many autumn flowering annual and perennial plants also attract butterflies. Try Coltness bedding dahlias. Single French marigolds like Naughty Marietta are a similar proposition.

Moths and bees

Although moths are largely nocturnal they do dance and play in the early evening, much to the gardener's enjoyment. Plant one of the older strains of flowering tobacco or nicotiana like Sensation near your sitting out area. Not only will you be delighted by their comings and goings, but entranced by the sweet fragrance of the tobacco flowers which heightens as darkness falls.

Rarely are the same activities noticed with other hardy night fragrant plants like night scented stock, but careful observation would be well rewarded as most night scented flowers are pollinated by moths.

Bees are more readily satisfied. Most popular garden plants prove an attraction. Herbs, however, are amongst their favourites. Colourful characters like the blue flowered borage, lilac blossomed marjoram and ultramarine hyssop. The thymes, lavender and rosemary are great magnets for bees as are the poached egg plant, catmint, sweet william and wallflowers, together with michaelmas daisies, candytuft and heather.

Native wild flowers

Wild flowers are an integral part of any wildlife corner. Nowadays seed companies offer a wide range of native species. Unfortunately, they are not the easiest of plants to grow, the majority preferring a more impoverished soil than most of us have in our gardens. A number depend on being grown from fresh seed and for the spring flowering kinds summer sowing is essential. Indeed, for most wild flowers this is a good time to sow, providing plants with an opportunity to develop sufficiently to be planted out in their permanent positions during autumn. They should then produce a good show the following spring and summer.

Most wild flower seeds benefit from being raised in trays in a frame but some, like the red and white campions, can be sown where they are to flower in a patch of prepared soil. This applies to the related catchfly and corn cockle too. The tufted vetch can also be established the same way. It is a charming plant, but take care that it does not develop territorial ambitions. A vigorous climber, it may attain a height of 6 ft. or so.

Restrained wild flowers

If you want to be certain that your wild flowers will not become invasive, then take a look at the primulas. Our native kinds embrace the primrose, oxlip and cowslip as well as a couple of high mountain species.

Few plants can compare with the common primrose for early spring beauty, its soft yellow blossoms twinkling like stars from a grassy hedge bottom. Cowslips and oxlips are plants for more open damp places. If you can provide a corner of uncut grass in which to naturalise them they will prosper. Do not sow seeds into grass, but raise small plants in trays first.

Apart from primulas, there are a number of near relatives which can be used to great effect. The lysimachias for example, particularly creeping Jenny, ideal for a damp shady corner, carpeting the soil in more or less evergreen foliage that during summer becomes studded with bright yellow buttercup-like blossoms.

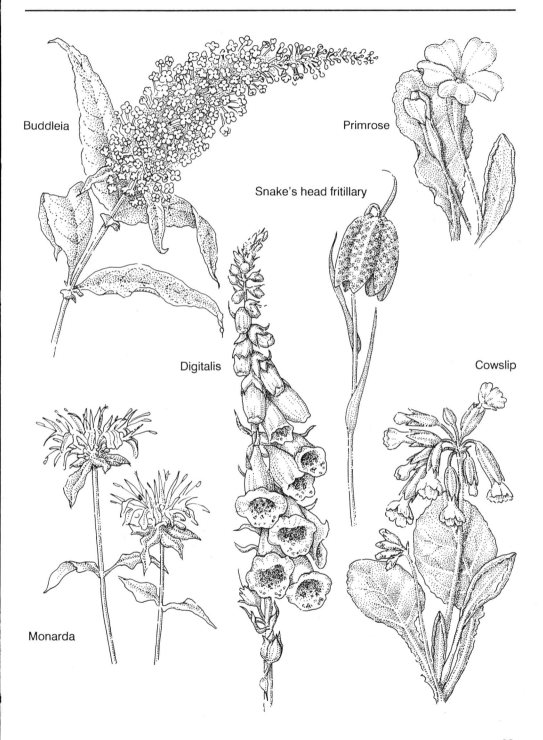

Buddleia

Primrose

Snake's head fritillary

Digitalis

Cowslip

Monarda

Rock garden construction

The site

A rock garden can be incorporated into any garden no matter what its size. Indeed, in a small area it is often the only form of gardening that will conform readily with such surroundings. Providing there is an open sunny spot, a rock garden can be successfully established.

Although it is not possible to produce exactly the same effect as that created by nature on the higher mountain slopes, or grow plants of quite the same excellence, we can go a long way towards doing so if we follow some basic principles.

The most important one is that a rock garden, no matter what size or shape, must be a moraine, not a mound of soil of dubious origin with rocks sticking out. A moraine in nature is an accumulation of rocks and other debris found alongside and at the base of a glacier. Such a moraine would not be too visually appealing, so we have to adapt it a little to ensure that it has all the qualities of the real thing, but at the same time is a tidy feature, easily managed.

Choosing the rocks

There are a number of different stones that are readily available to gardeners. These vary greatly in texture and colour. The choice that is made is a very personal one. However, it must be said that stones from an area always look most appealing when used in that locality. Imported stone, unless very carefully placed, usually looks quite alien. Northern rocks are mostly the millstone grits of Yorkshire and the water washed limestones and blue-green slates of Westmorland.

Other important rocks are the pinkish Forest of Dean limestone, north Norfolk carstone and Sussex sandstone, the latter being orange-red or rich brown.

Sorting and placing the rocks

Once delivered to your garden, sort out the rocks and determine the best faces, and where appropriate, the line of strata. It is important to present the most natural and appealing aspects of each rock.

The rocks that are to form the base of the rock garden should be selected and placed in position to create what almost amounts to a retaining wall which outlines the contours of the feature. As far as possible a rock garden should look as if it is growing out of the landscape rather than sitting on it. Select a

1 The site

Mark out the area of the rock garden and remove the top soil. Ensure that the site is well drained.

2 Laying the base

Build up the rock feature in layers. Fill the area between the rocks with free-draining compost. Rake out the bedding material.

rock to provide the focal point. This is usually one of the largest rocks and is known as the key stone. It exposes at least two faces, often more, and it is from this that the remainder of the rock outcrop will develop.

When placing rocks ensure that the strata runs in the same direction. A stone placed upside down or on its edge is a constant source of irritation. If there are slight colour variations ensure that there is sufficient space between the rocks to allow for liberal planting. Two rocks of slightly varying colour which are separated by plant foliage are no longer noticeably different.

Soft stones, particularly limestone, require very careful placing, whereas harder ones such as granite and slate are almost totally devoid of a clearly defined strata and can be used more freely. However, it is important to use all one type of stone and it should be proper rock, not an accumulation of broken concrete or hardcore.

The only kind of artificial material that can be permitted is that known as hypertufa, a soft rock substitute which can be easily made by any handy gardener. Dig several holes roughly the size and shape of the desired rocks in a vacant part of the garden, perhaps on the vegetable plot. Prepare a mixture of one part cement, one part sand and two parts finely sieved peat, adding water until it is of a creamy texture. Pour the agglomeration into the excavations and allow it to set before re-excavating some very fine economically priced rocks.

Filling the cavities

Once the key basal stones of the rock garden have been laid the area between should be filled with a mixture of about two thirds stone and one third gritty soil. Where they are not likely to be exposed to view old bricks and broken roof tiles make excellent filling if camouflaged with a good depth of stony soil. Old tin cans and similar rubbish must not be used, for although they provide good drainage for a couple of years, they eventually rot away and cause areas of the rock garden to subside.

Having laid the base, filled the cavities, and generally formed a solid plateau, further stones can be lifted into position and the process repeated until the formation is of the desired shape and height. When completed, pockets between rocks that are to house species of plants with particular specialised requirements can be excavated and a suitable compost introduced.

3 Placing the rocks

Each layer should be set back slightly from the one below. Make adequate provision for planting.

4 Planting

Plant so that there is interest for as long a season as possible. Dwarf conifers add permanent structure to the feature.

Planting and maintenance

It is advantageous to plant during early spring, just before fresh growth begins. The plants then establish much quicker.

Plant selection

Conifers are the backbone of the rock garden, providing evergreen foliage of a varied and cheerful hue and giving character to a barren landscape during winter. True miniature kinds which grow at the rate of an inch or so every year are all very well, but they take a lifetime to become fully effective.

Try planting slow growing conifers instead. These are of dwarf habit, but outgrow their positions after a dozen years and can then be replaced by young plants. A favourite is Ellwood's cypress, *Chamaecyparis lawsoniana* Ellwoodii, a small upright conifer of narrow conical shape with beautiful glaucous green feathery foliage. *Thuja* Rheingold grows into a big golden-yellow ball while the tiny Christmas tree-like *Picea albertiana* Conica makes a symmetrical mound of fresh green foliage. Prostrate conifers come into their own towards the edge of the rock garden. Amongst the most useful is the steely-blue Juniperus Blue Star with a neat carpeting habit.

Dwarf flowering shrubs are invaluable too, but should be used sparingly. The delightful *Rhododendron repens* with deep crimson bells and evergreen foliage scarcely six inches high is ideal for a cool position on a north-facing slope while the tiny red flowered *Spiraea bullata* Nana seems to grow happily anywhere. The spectacular dwarf broom *Cytisus kewensis* needs a sunny spot and makes a picture of unrivalled beauty planted just above a rock where its sprays of creamy blossoms cascade over the face.

Rock roses or heliothemums need full sun and a free-draining soil, rewarding with a summer-long display of papery flowers in the most exquisite shades. Alpine pinks enjoy similar conditions and fill the air with a delicious fragrance. All will form hummocks of green or silvery-grey foliage and are wreathed in delicate blossoms. The maiden pink, Dianthus deltoides, its white form Alba and the cherry-red Brilliancy are superb.

The alpine aster Aster alpinus is of similar constitution, thriving in adversity and filling a pocket with coarse green leaves sprinkled with starry blossoms of deep lilac-blue sporting bright yellow centres. The alpine poppy, *Papaver alpinum*, is an excellent companion, its delicate silvery grey foliage surmounted by fragrant nodding chalices of orange, yellow or pink. The innumerable saxifrages delight with their well starched flowers above neat foliage.

Deep purple aubretia, pink and white arabis, together with yellow alyssum should not be overlooked, for, although somewhat invasive, they are useful in the early development of the rock garden. All spread quickly giving an early appearance of maturity. As other inhabitants become established, vigorous kinds can be removed and replaced with better behaved relatives like the dainty carmine flowered *Arabis* Spring Charm, the gorgeous semi-double Bengal hybrid strain of aubretia and the tiny canary-yellow *Alyssum idaeum*.

Close growing and creeping plants are very important in creating a natural looking rock feature. Amongst suitable plants we have the tight golden mats of *Arenaria caespitosa* Aurea, the ground hugging sedums, like the yellow-flowered *Sedum acre* and the purple-leafed *S. spathulifolium* Purpureum, each excellent subjects for flowing down crevices. Meanwhile rupturewort *Herniaria glabra* provides soil cover in niches where dwarf bulbs have been planted.

Miniature bulbs

Establish liberal plantings of dwarf narcissus, tiny scillas, the species crocus and reticulate iris. Snakeshead lilies, snowdrops, grape hyacinths and botanical tulips are also suitable and will increase annually.

Maintenance

A rock garden is not difficult to maintain if kept weed-free. Remove faded blossoms regularly and after flowering provide a pinch of bonemeal in the centre of each clump of plants to sustain stable growth. Never use a high nitrogen or quick acting fertiliser as this can distort a plant's growth.

Take care to ensure that during autumn leaves do not accumulate in pockets on the rock garden. In early spring protect succulent young shoots from slugs by the regular distribution of slug bait.

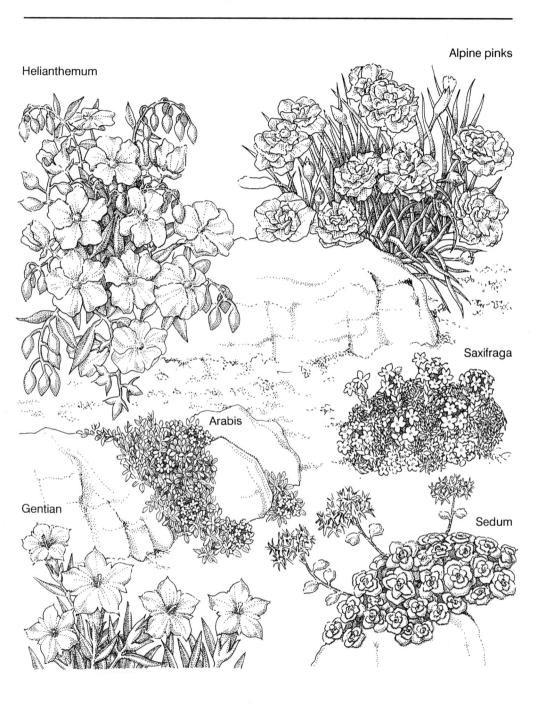

Helianthemum

Alpine pinks

Saxifraga

Arabis

Gentian

Sedum

Garden pool construction

A garden pool is a tremendous asset, introducing movement and life as well as new sounds. To be successful it should be sited in full sun, away from buildings and trees and in a lower part of the landscape.

Pool liners

Pool liners are the most versatile of pool construction materials and are now available in a diversity of materials and colours. They are essentially sheets of waterproof material that are used to line an excavation, thus providing a waterproof skin.

Those made from polythene are the cheapest, often available in a blue or stone colour, and enable everyone to have a water garden. They have their limitations though, for not only have they little elasticity, which makes them more difficult to instal, but they also have a tendency to perish if not carefully managed. This occurs between the water surface and ground level, the narrow band of polythene that is exposed through water-evaporation becoming bleached and weakened by sunlight, ultimately cracking and separating.

Rubber and PVC liners are more permanent, but also considerably more expensive. The rubber kinds are the same material as used by farmers for irrigation lagoons, while the PVC ones are often reinforced with a terylene web to improve their burst resistance.

In order to calculate the size of liner required for a regular pool, measure the length x twice the maximum depth by the width x twice the maximum depth. The liner for a pool of irregular shape should be calculated upon the dimensions of a rectangle that embraces the most distant parts of the excavation.

Once the pool has been excavated the hole should be scoured for any sharp objects that may puncture the liner once it is installed and water has been added. Cover the floor of the pool with a generous layer of sand to act as a cushion, and on stony soils pad the walls using the fleece available for the purpose from garden centres.

Installing a liner

Polythene pool liners have to be placed in the excavation and moulded to its contours before water is added as they have little elasticity. This can be aided on a warm sunny day if the liner is spread out for a few hours before installation. It then becomes much more supple.

Conversely, rubber and PVC liners are spread out evenly over the hole and water is

1 Excavation

A strong plank on edge used with a spirit level is the most satisfactory means of keeping the pool level.

2 Protection

Check for sharp objects then cover the floor of the pool with a generous layer of sand to act as a cushion.

poured into the centre. The outspread liner is held in position by a number of rocks or stones which secure it to the edge. As the weight of water starts to pull the liner down, these weights are gradually released so that the liner can fit snugly into the excavation.

As the pool fills, the wrinkles that appear should be carefully smoothed out or disguised for once the excavation is full of water they are impossible to deal with. Once the liner has been installed to everyone's satisfaction the surplus material around the top can be cut away, just sufficient being allowed to remain for fastening to the ground with paving or rockwork.

Preformed pools

Preformed pools are usually made out of PVC or fibreglass, although some are produced from vacuum-formed plastic. Ensure that the one that is chosen is of sufficient depth to accommodate a waterlily and submerged plants and see that the marginal shelves are sufficiently wide to take a standard planting basket.

When installing a pre-formed pool measure the external maximum dimensions of the pool and then dig a hole sufficiently large to embrace the whole structure. This is usually rectangular and slightly larger than the pool to allow room for backfilling.

The pre-formed pool is placed in position, level from end to end and side to side. Where there are discrepancies in depth, the shallow end is supported on bricks to bring it level. Levels are very important and a strong plank on edge used with a spirit level is the most satisfactory means of keeping the pool level.

If the soil that has been excavated is in a good friable condition it can be used for backfilling, but where this is not so, river sand or pea gravel are satisfactory free-flowing substitutes.

Moving water

Moving water provides an added dimension to the garden, adding sparkle and sound, but places restrictions on what is grown in the pool. Few aquatic plants enjoy constantly moving water, so a choice must be made in the small pool as to whether it is a fountain or waterlilies that are to be enjoyed.

Only in the largest pool can both be accommodated satisfactorily. With modern technology it is relatively simple to have moving water, either as a fountain, a waterfall, or both. Submersible pumps that can be run from mains electricity have revolutionised and dramatically reduced the costs of providing such a feature.

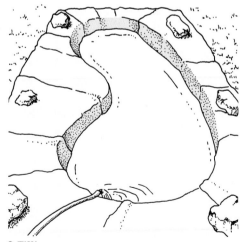

3 Filling

Spread the liner over the excavation, weigh it down with rocks and fill with water from a hosepipe.

4 Edging

Cut away the surplus liner, leaving enough for fastening to the ground. Edge the rim of the pool with stones.

Planting and maintenance

In planting a garden pool a whole new underwater world is being created in which plants, fish and snails depend upon one another to provide the basic requirements necessary for their continued existence.

Creating a balance

Submerged oxygenating plants replace the oxygen that has been lost to respiration and compete with slimes, algae and other primitive forms of plant life which turn the water thick and green by using up all the available mineral salts.

Plants with floating foliage assist by shading the surface of the water, making life intolerable for any of the green water discolouring algae which tries to dwell beneath them. The marginal plants provide the necessary colour to make the pool a continual source of delight.

When planning the planting, bear in mind the quantity of each type of plant necessary to create a balance then select within these limits those that have a particular personal appeal. At least one third of the surface area of the pool, excluding the marginal shelves, should be covered with floating foliage. This need not be composed entirely of floating aquatics, for waterlilies and other deep water aquatics provide considerable cover with their floating leaves.

Initial stocking with submerged oxygenating plants is recommended at one to every 2 sq.ft. of surface area, evenly distributed over the pool floor, and with fish, a maximum 6 ins. long to every square foot of surface area, although 2 ins. to the same surface area is more sensible. Snails of the flat curled ramshorn type may be introduced liberally, as may marginal plants.

Waterlilies

Waterlilies are usually the first priority when planting a pool, and this is hardly surprising since these gorgeous subjects provide a dazzling display of flowers from early June until the first autumn frosts and are available in almost every shape, size and colour imaginable. Planting season for waterlilies and all other aquatic plants is from April until August, the plants being established in baskets of good clean garden soil with just their 'noses' protruding above the surface.

When collecting soil prior to planting, it is important to avoid getting any old leaves or weeds mixed in with it as these will only decompose and foul the water. Soil from land that has recently been dressed with artificial fertiliser should be similarly avoided.

Once the plant is installed in the basket, the soil should be covered with about half an inch of washed pebbles in order to prevent fish from disturbing the compost and dirtying the water. It is also advantageous to remove all the adult leaves from waterlilies and similar lily-like aquatics before planting as they give buoyancy to the plants and are capable of lifting them out of the baskets.

The maintenance of plants

In spring established aquatic plants should be fertilised using sachets of prepared water plant fertiliser pushed into the compost in the baskets next to the plants so that nutrients are released where they will be used and not in the water. It is also possible to use bonemeal 'pills' in the same way. These are small balls of clay soil with bonemeal mixed into them and serve the same purpose without polluting the water.

During autumn waterlilies and other deep water aquatics die back. Most marginal plants behave like border perennials and need cutting back, but be careful not to cut hollow stemmed varieties beneath water level. If the stems become full of water the plants will usually perish.

Most floating aquatics form turions or winter buds during the autumn and then fall to the bottom of the pool, remaining there until the spring sunshine warms the water again. They will then return to the surface.

Caring for fish

Most gardeners like to feed fish, though they do not really require it once a pool has become established. Feed a good quality fish food, scattering no more on the surface than the fish can eat in twenty minutes. If the pool has a minimum depth of at least one and a half feet in one part they are unlikely to come to any harm in the winter months. It is not cold that kills fish, but the trapping of noxious gases by prolonged ice cover. A pool heater is ideal, but where this is not possible keep an ice-free opening by periodically placing a pan of boiling water on the surface, allowing it to melt through.

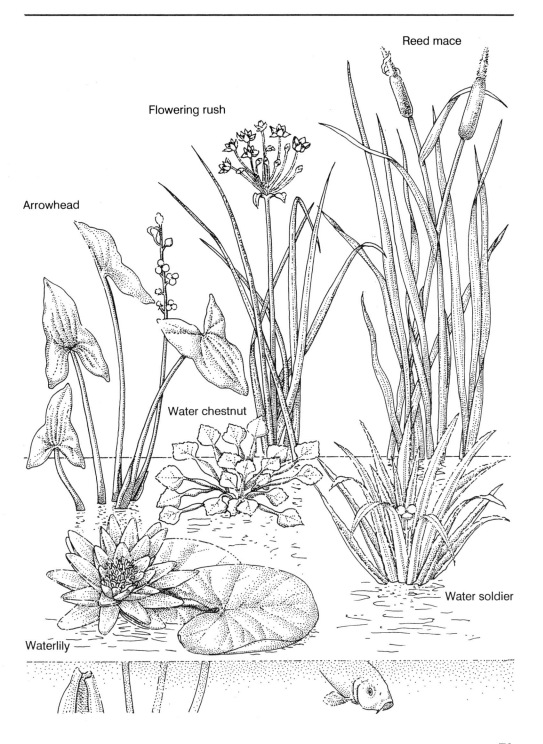

Reed mace

Flowering rush

Arrowhead

Water chestnut

Waterlily

Water soldier

Herbs and vegetables

There are some vegetables that do not conveniently fit into any particular category and are treated separately on the vegetable plot. Herbs are a similar proposition, usually being grown more successfully in poorer soil in a hot sunny spot, or else in tubs and planters on the patio.

Onions and leeks

Both onions and leeks are very popular traditional northern vegetables, both of easy culture for ordinary garden use but demanding special skills to attain the quality demanded for the show bench.

Seed of either is sown under glass during early spring. It should be sown thinly and lightly covered with compost. Within ten days or a fortnight the seedlings will emerge and look rather like fine grass, except that they will be crooked, with the upper part of the seed leaf turned down.

Pricking out should ideally take place while the seedlings look like small shepherd's crooks. Space them out evenly in seed trays with a generous depth of compost so that good root development can take place. Allow them to remain in the trays until they are planted out during late spring or early summer. If you wish to grow show specimens then it is more usual to transplant them into individual pots as soon as the plants are big enough.

Leeks and onions both benefit from a rich organic soil and so plenty of well rotted manure or garden compost should be dug in during the autumn. The soil will then have plenty of time to settle down. This is particularly important for onions as they require a very firm bed.

Plant onions and leeks in rows 1ft apart with 6 ins. between plants. With leeks it is usual to make a hole and drop the plant in up to the base of its leaves. On light soil leeks can be grown in trenches and then earthed up as autumn approaches. These techniques ensure a long white blanch. Cul-

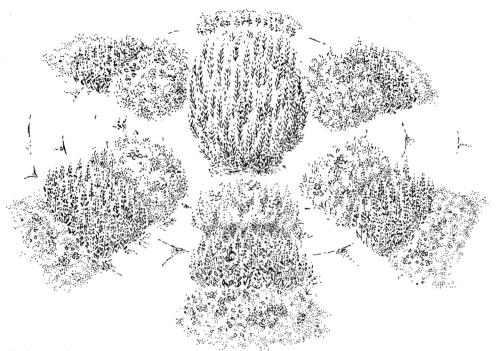

Herb wheel

A herb wheel garden planted with, from centre, rosemary, cotton lavender, hyssop and golden lemon thyme.

tivation consists of the regular hoeing of the rows and keeping an eye open for pests and diseases. Onions are harvested when their foliage starts to turn brown but leeks are lifted as and when required.

Marrows, courgettes and squashes

Seed of all these vegetables is sown during April or early May with the protection of a frame or window ledge. Do not sow them any earlier or else the rapidly growing plants will become difficult to control. They do not tolerate any frost and so must not be planted out until the early part of June. Resenting disturbance, they are best raised individually in pots, being planted out in a very rich moisture-retentive soil where there is plenty of room to spread. Even a modest bush form of marrow will occupy 3 ft. by 3 ft.

Apart from regular weeding and ensuring that they receive sufficient moisture, cultivation is straightforward. All produce male and female flowers and for a crop to set properly it is vital that fertilisation takes place. When the first flowers are produced pick the open male flower and push it into the waiting female one thereby transferring the pollen. The female flower is easily recognised as it has a tiny marrow or squash behind it.

Once fertilised, the fruits swell quickly. Courgettes are harvested when immature, but marrows, squashes and pumpkins are not gathered until fully developed.

Herbs

Herbs are increasing in popularity enormously, being grown on window ledges and in patio planters as well as the open garden. Of all the culinary plants, herbs adapt themselves best to this restricted form of cultivation. In addition to popular herbs such as thyme, parsley and sage, there are a whole host of others that are not difficult to grow in our cool climate. The wonderful celery-scented lovage, the giant angelica and strongly aromatic summer savory. Winter savory, rue, marjoram and sorrel are all easily grown too, providing that you give them an open sunny situation.

Some herbs, like dill and coriander, are annual and need replacing each year. Sow the seeds where they are to mature during the spring. Once the seedlings emerge, thin them out, allowing plenty of space for development. Most plants need to be between 6 ins. and 9 ins. apart. The thinned seedlings of most herbs should be discarded as they rarely transplant successfully.

Take care with some of the invasive perennial kinds like the mints. These are best planted in tubs sunk into the soil thereby reducing their spread. Left unchecked, they will swamp the herb garden. Watch out for those that produce seed as well. If fading flower heads remain untended self-sown seedlings may become a problem. Removing spent flower stems also improves the quality of the foliage.

Given an open sunny position most herbs prosper with little attention. Slugs occasionally chew emerging shoots and aphid attacks are a possibility, but if a good cultural routine is followed there should be no major problem with pests or diseases.

Herb wheel

A cartwheel herb garden is traditionally made using a cartwheel placed on well cultivated soil, individual herb varieties being planted into the soil in the gaps between the spokes. Nowadays the traditional design is adapted so that the effect is similar to that of a cartwheel, the divisions being created by stones, paving or bricks. This has the great advantage of creating much larger planting areas for individual herbs.

Care should be taken to ensure that only herbs of modest stature are planted otherwise the design becomes distorted. A taller species such as rosemary can be planted in the centre, but herbs like cotton lavender, hyssop and lemon thyme can be planted progressively downwards to the edge.

Drying herbs

Apart from being used fresh a considerable number of herbs are suitable for drying. Gather young foliage at, or just before, the flowering stage on a warm day when the leaves are absolutely dry. Large leafed kinds can have the leaves removed from the stalks, but small leafed varieties can be dried as they are. When dry and crisp the foliage should be crushed with a rolling pin and then stored in jars until required.

Salad vegetables

There are many vegetables which are also classified as salads to be found elsewhere in this book. The ones noted here are the salads of the open vegetable garden.

Lettuce

There are two main groups of lettuce – cabbage and cos. The cabbage lettuce are the small rounded ones that form a hard heart, while the cos are tall and upright. The cabbage section is many times larger than the cos and is itself divided into two separate groups; the crisp hearted and soft or butterhead varieties.

The former group is characterised by that old favourite Webbs's Wonderful, known with affection even by non-gardeners as Webbs.

Many improved and different sized varieties of the same habit and texture are now available to the home gardener and these are popularly referred to as Icebergs.

The finest amongst these is the small, compact variety Windermere. This forms a hard solid head no more than 4 ins. in diameter and produces a minimum of useless outer leaves. It is also slow to run to seed, even in hot weather, and is only equalled in this section by the slightly larger, disease resistant Avoncrisp. Others worth considering, but much bulkier and leafier, include Iceberg and Great Lakes.

There are more butterhead varieties than crisp hearted sorts. These are typified by All The Year Round, a reliable kind that can be sown with success at most seasons of the year. Avondefiance is a darker green and mildew resistant, while the tiny Tom Thumb is a variety for the small household to grow. The compact hard heart of this variety is about the size of a tennis ball.

Fortune and Suzan are two good butterhead varieties that resemble All The Year Round. If you like to add a little variation to your salads, then there is the firm hearted, reddish leafed Continuity, or the loose-leafed Salad Bowl which is one of the best cut and come again lettuces.

All these varieties can be sown from March until July in the open ground. Do not be tempted to grow full rows, rather sow a pinch of seed at a time at regular intervals. This will ensure that you have a continuity of fresh lettuce.

While many gardeners successfully transplant lettuce during the early spring, it is not to be recommended for the summer months. All lettuce sown now should continue to grow in situ, the seedlings being thinned out to their final spacings when large enough to handle. Transplanted seedlings usually run to seed without forming a proper heart.

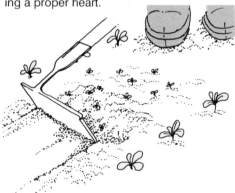

1 Sowing

Sow lettuce in seed drills in open ground from March to July.

2 Growing

Allow to grow in situ.

Outdoor cucumbers

The ridge or outdoor cucumber has always been considered to be the poor mans' greenhouse cucumber, but many gardeners consider the flavour and texture of these shorter knobbly fruits to be superior to anything produced in the frame or glasshouse. For the best results the seed should be sown individually in small pots in an ordinary seed compost during late April in a frame or greenhouse. Young plants with a couple of rough leaves will then be ready for planting out towards the end of May when hopefully all danger of frost has passed. If a frost is forecast after the plants are in position, it is a simple matter to drop a Kilner jar over each one for the night to afford some measure of protection.

The former mystique surrounding the cultivation of ridge cucumbers which developed during the early years of this century has now largely disappeared. None but the most old-fashioned gardener would consider growing his cucumbers on a ridge. A well manured soil on the flat is quite adequate, in fact it is probably better as water is more likely to be retained than when sprayed on a ridge. Once established and growing strongly nothing more need be done except for a mulch of decayed manure or well rotted garden compost around the base of the plant to conserve moisture and provide a cool root run.

There are numerous varieties of ridge cucumber available which are suited to differ-

ent purposes. Stockwood Ridge and Long Green Ridge are traditional varieties producing short or medium length fruits that are knobbly and prickly but of delicious flavour. Perfection and Nadir bear longer and similar fruits, like their greenhouse cousins, while the new Burpless hybrids such as Burpless Tasty Green can be cut lengthways and eaten without peeling in exactly the same manner as celery.

Radish

Radishes are the easiest vegetable to grow. Sow them directly into drills from March until August and harvest six weeks later. Being such quick maturing plants they are extremely useful for intercropping between long standing crops such as Brussels sprouts and broccoli, occupying the soil between for such a short period that it makes no difference to the cultivation or behaviour of the other crops.

Sow seed very thinly in the rows as radish cannot be transplanted. It can be thinned, and this is usually necessary, but it is wasteful to throw away large numbers of seedlings. There are innumerable varieties to choose from, but French Breakfast is one of the best known of the longer rooted varieties while Scarlet Globe and Cherry Belle are popular round kinds.

Spring onions

Little need be said here about the cultivation of spring onions except that you grow them in the same way as bulb onions, but leave them to develop where they are. It is the variety that is different, White Lisbon being the most useful summer kind while Winter White Lisbon is sown in September for an early spring harvest.

In a confined space chives can be used as an alternative for early spring onions. These can be grown in a permanent patch either in the herb bed or in a corner of the vegetable garden. Summer crops can be supplemented with bunching onions. These are raised from seed sown directly in the open ground during March. They produce clusters of onions rather like giant chives. The most popular variety is Kyoto.

3 Thinning

Thin out seedlings to their final spacings when large enough to handle.

Root vegetables

Rootcrops are those that produce a crop from beneath ground whether they be true roots or tubers. All demand a fertile free-draining soil and an open sunny situation.

Carrots

Carrots can be sown in succession from March until late June in a finely prepared seed bed in soil which has not recently been manured. Sow the seed in drills about 1 in. deep in rows a 1 ft. apart. If carrot fly is known to be troublesome a seed dressing can be mixed with the seed before distribution along the rows.

After ten days or a fortnight seedlings will appear looking rather like rows of very fine grass. At this stage the soil between the rows should be hoed to destroy any weed seedlings coming up. A couple of weeks later, when the seedlings are an inch or so high, they can be thinned to about an inch apart. After thinning, unwanted seedlings should be put on the compost heap. Never leave them lying between rows as the aroma from the bruised foliage attracts the carrot fly.

When the roots have swollen to a good finger size remove every other one and use them raw in salads or else cooked as tender young carrots. This size carrot freezes particularly well whole for use later in the year when young carrots have long been forgotten. A further pulling of alternate roots can

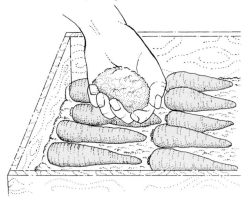

Storing root vegetables
Vegetables keep well if the roots are lifted during autumn when mature and stored in clamps or boxes of sand.

be made three weeks later, the remainder being left in the ground until mature.

Readiness for lifting with maincrop carrots can be taken as the stage at which the carrot has reached when the foliage is just starting to yellow. This colour should be yellow, not rusty red or mauve, for the latter colouration, accompanied by a wilting of the foliage, is a sure sign of carrot fly. Pulling one or two roots to inspect for maggots will reveal the extent of the infestation. When it has reached this stage nothing can be done but take precautions for the next season.

Beet

There are three kinds of beet. The globe shaped varieties with which most gardeners are familiar, the long-rooted kinds which are used for storing and the leaf beets which include Swiss chard and perpetual spinach.

Beet can be sown from April onwards in drills an inch deep with 18 ins. between the rows. Sow thinly as each 'seed' is really a capsule containing several seeds and when germinating will produce a cluster of seedlings. Protect freshly sown seed with wire pea guards as sparrows delight in pulling at emerging seedlings. Once they touch the tops of the guards it can be assumed that they will grow on safely uncovered. Hoe between the rows and thin the young plants to 3 ins. apart. Early sowings can be left like this, just hoeing regularly to keep the soil open, until the roots almost touch in the rows when they can be harvested. Globe shaped varieties for winter keeping should be treated similarly, the tender young roots being thinned from 3 ins. apart to 6 ins. between plants, the thinnings being used for pickling or deep freezing.

Regular hoeing should then continue until autumn, or when the foliage assumes deep purple or bronze tints whichever is the sooner, and the roots lifted.

All beets are tender and subject to bruising if handled roughly. Leaves should be twisted off to prevent bleeding and subsequent discolouring of the roots.

Parsnips

Any soil not recently manured will grow good parsnips if thoroughly prepared, but a light sandy soil of good depth generally produces the best quality roots. Well dug heavy soils will yield reasonable sized roots, but for the giants beloved of most gardeners it is necessary to prepare stations at about 12 ins. intervals in the rows. These are holes that are created with an iron rod or broom handle pushed into the soil and moved about, afterwards being filled with good quality compost.

For normal sowings on medium to light soils nothing as elaborate need be done, nor on heavy soil if you are satisfied with short broad shouldered roots like overgrown carrots. Sow the seed in drills any time during February and March, the rows being 18 ins. apart and the plants eventually thinned to 6 to 8 ins. in the rows.

Parsnip seed is thin and papery, like small slivers of tissue, and because it takes four or five weeks to germinate is particularly susceptible to rotting in the soil in conditions of excessive dampness. On lighter soils a sowing can be made as soon as the ground is workable. As a long season of growth is desirable, the sooner the seed is sown, within reason, the better.

There are no early or maincrops with parsnips, for all come to maturity during October and November and are ready to use when their foliage dies back.

Swede

Swedes should be sown during May in drills about 1 in. deep with 18 ins. between rows. When large enough to handle the seedlings can be thinned to 1ft apart, unwanted plants being put on the compost heap. Although the swede is technically a brassica it resents disturbance and will not produce an edible root even if it survives transplanting.

Most swedes keep well if the roots are lifted during autumn when mature and stored in clamps or boxes of sand. The old tops should be cut or twisted off and the 'tail' or vestige of tap root removed.

Turnip

Like the swede, the turnip is a root crop which is also a brassica. It can be sown outdoors any time from early March until September, but is most useful when grown from a late summer sowing for use during the winter. Sow the seeds in rows 15 ins. apart, thinning the young plants to 6 ins. apart as soon as they are large enough to handle.

Potatoes

Seed potatoes are something of a misnomer, for it is not the seed of the potato that is planted, but small selected tubers. The importance of buying first quality Ministry certified 'seed' cannot be emphasised too much, for it takes no more effort to plant and tend a good potato crop than it does one started from the remnants of last year's harvest, yet the results obtained from using quality 'seed' are vastly superior.

It is advantageous to spread out freshly purchased seed potatoes in boxes for 'chitting' or sprouting in a cool airy place.

This is particularly valuable with early varieties, for proper chitting can advance the harvest by as much as two or three weeks at a time when new potatoes are very expensive.

After two or three weeks the shoots will be growing strongly. Ensure that they have plenty of light or else they will become very leggy. They should eventually be reduced to the strongest two shoots which are then allowed to grow an inch or so long before the tubers are planted.

Early potatoes are usually planted towards the end of March, while second early and maincrop sorts are left until April. These will provide a harvest from late June onwards.

Plant the potatoes in trenches that are 6 ins. deep and the width of a spade. Place the tubers 9 ins. apart for early varieties, but 1 ft apart for all the others. Cover them with soil, ensuring that the rows are no closer than 2 ft.

As the foliage is produced earth up the plants. This is done by creating a ridge of soil from that removed from between the rows. The taller the ridges become, the heavier the crop is likely to be providing that it is kept well watered.

Early varieties can be lifted as soon as the flowers fade, but maincrop sorts should not be dug until the foliage has turned yellow and died back.

Legumes

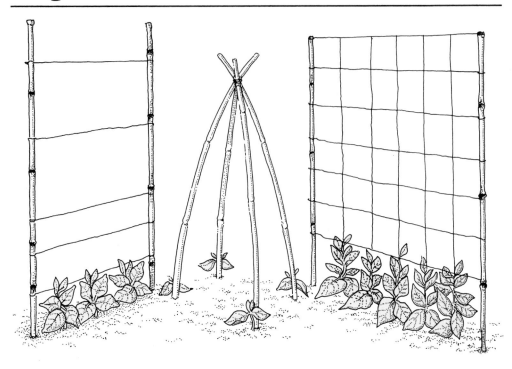

Supporting legumes

Growing beans on wires and canes, up inverted poles and nets.

The pea and bean family are very important for the northern gardener. Reliable and of easy cultivation, they have the added benefit of fixing nitrogen from the air in nodules on their roots. When the crop is removed the roots should remain in the soil, being dug in to provide added nitrogen for the next crop, ideally a leafy vegetable like cabbage which will benefit from this bonus.

Broad beans

Broad bean seeds are sown during February and March in flat drills 4 or 5 ins wide, the seeds being placed in a double row with a seed dropped in the centre of every group of four. Spare seeds can be sown at the end of the row and transplanted into any gaps evident when a couple of inches high.

There are three types of broad bean; long pod, Windsor, and short pod. The first two types are further divided into white and green seeded. Some gardeners believe that the green seed varieties have a superior

flavour. They certainly freeze better than their white counterparts, but both grow well and are identical in other respects.

There are many varieties from which to choose, but for a very early sowing few can surpass Aquadulce for hardiness and early maturity. It is of the long pod type and white seeded, as is Meteor, a heavy cropping kind with slightly shorter broad pods.

Exhibition Longpod and Colossal are intended for the show bench, but are good garden varieties as well. For gardeners with a freezer the green seeded Masterpiece Green Longpod is the one to select. The Windsor varieties are not quite as resilient as the long pod kinds, but atone for this by their sweetness and succulence. The routine care of broadbeans consists of regular hoeing between the rows, which in the case of all maincrop varieties should be about 2 ft. apart. In exposed areas a little soil can be mounded up around the base of the plants to give extra support.

Peas

There are several different types of peas, all of which can be grown in much the same way as suggested for broad beans. The main categories of pea for the northern garden are early, second early, maincrop and petit pois, the latter being very small seeded sweet varieties. Within these groups there are a multiplicity of kinds of different habits and dispositions. Select carefully from the seed catalogue, bearing in mind the kind of garden that you have. Obviously it is folly to attempt a tall growing kind in a windy situation or in the salt laden breezes of a coastal garden, but these very same varieties can considerably increase the weight of crop per foot of row in a sheltered suburban garden where space is scarce and the only way is upwards. In small fenced gardens or courtyards suprisingly heavy crops of peas can be reaped from tall varieties like The Senator or Lord Chancellor growing against a fence or up sticks.

Shorter varieties such as Kelvedon Wonder and Feltham First do better in exposed situations, or for cultivation under cloches where their smaller stature is vital. Given the choice with a medium or heavy soil, or else one that has an abundance of moisture retaining organic matter incorporated in it, select the tallest growing variety available for the particular period of time over which you would like to pick the crop. The weight of peas yielded per foot of row will greatly exceed that of a shorter variety, although the latter can grow in rows that are closer together. As a general rule a 4 ft. high pea will produce a better return on its space than a 2 ft. high variety.

Early varieties of pea are usually round seeded, while later ones are wrinkle seeded or marrow-fat peas. The former are particularly hardy and suitable for very early sowings. The wrinkle seeded are not quite so resilient but of better flavour owing to their higher sugar content.

Grow peas in much the same way as broad beans, except that any pea sticks or netting to be used for support should be put in place as soon as the seedlings push through the soil. At this time they are particularly vulnerable to attack by sparrows and pigeons, so it is prudent to cover emerging seedlings with wire pea guards until they are a couple of inches high. Otherwise cultivation is confined to keeping the rows weed-free and watching out for signs of mildew. This is a white fungal deposit which appears on the foliage causing disfigurement. The regular use of a systemic fungicide until a month before harvesting keeps peas clear of this nuisance.

Runner beans

Sow the seed of runner beans in the positions in which the plants are to grow. Usually they are planted in a similar manner to broad beans in shallow drills, the seeds being sown individually 4 ins. apart in double rows that are 2 ft. apart. This means that when staked the poles can lean inwards to form a shape that is an inverted 'V' in profile, the tops of all the poles or stakes being lashed to strong canes or sticks that lie in a continuous horizontal plane.

If nets are used a similar method can be adopted, the nets being fastened to a light framework of poles, although equally good results can be obtained when the nets are erected in a conventional manner, providing the supporting stakes and wire are strong enough to carry the weight of foliage.

Growth is rapid and within four or five weeks the supports will be smothered in foliage and interspersed with flowers. When the top of the supports have been reached at 4 or 5 ft. the growing points of the plants should be removed to encourage them to blossom more heavily.

Once the young beans have formed they should be carefully watched and when large enough to use should be picked over daily. A good guide as to their readiness is to watch the flattened beans for any sign of lumpiness. Immediately any slight distending of the skin takes place the pod should be picked before it has a chance to go stringy and bitter.

Most gardeners grow the scarlet flowered kinds or runner bean typified by varieties like Scarlet Emperor and Streamline. These and old stagers like Prizewinner and Kelvedon Marvel have very few differences except in earliness and pod length.

Leaf vegetables

There are numerous leafy vegetables that can be grown in the home garden. Most are very hardy and not difficult to cultivate in soil that is in good heart.

Cabbages

Cabbages can be roughly divided into two groups; the ones that may be sown during spring and early summer, and those that are commonly known as spring cabbages which are raised from an autumn sowing.

Generally, varieties are clearly divided into these two categories, although some, like Wheeler's Imperial, can be sown at both times.

There are also the crinkly kinds formerly known as Curled Garden Cole which we now call savoy cabbage and the comparatively recently popularised Chinese cabbage which is more akin to a coarse-leafed cos lettuce.

Then there are the red or pickling varieties. These are becoming increasingly popular for cooking as well as preserving.

Transplanting seedlings

Plant seedlings on an overcast day when there is less chance of the young plants being checked by the sun. The use of a dibber can be recommended on lighter soils.

Calabrese and broccoli

The seed of all calabrese varieties should be sown at the same time irrespective of the period it takes for them to mature. The middle of March is ideal, the seed being sown in close rows in a seed bed for planting out as soon as big enough to handle. Five or six weeks will elapse before they are large enough to move to their permanent quarters, when they should be planted about two feet apart with three feet between rows. This wide planting is necessary as the plants are substantial when fully grown.

Sprouting broccoli is treated in an identical manner, but is generally sown a month or so later. Further differences in culture apply to the long winter period which the sprouting broccoli unflinchingly endures. A dressing of sulphate of potash amongst the plants at half an ounce per square yard in the autumn toughens them up for the winter while the addition of stakes in exposed districts prevents the top heavy plants being blown over.

Brussels sprouts

Seed of most varieties should be sown during March, although the spring maturing kinds can be left until April. Sowing follows along the lines advocated for broccoli, the rows being close together and the plants moved as soon as large enough to handle. Only very sturdy plants should be selected and these planted according to variety in rows two or three feet apart with two or three feet between rows.

Summer cultivation consists of keeping down the weeds and ensuring that the plants do not suffer from wind-rock. This is likely to happen during the autumn in times of high winds when the somewhat top-heavy plants are swayed backwards and forwards loosening the roots and causing blowing or rosetting of the buttons.

Cauliflowers

There are basically three groups of cauliflowers. The first are the summer heading types which are sown in a frame during September and October for planting out with protection early in the year, or else sown in gentle heat in a glasshouse during January and February for open ground planting in March. These are followed by the autumn heading kinds which are sown during April directly in the open ground.

Finally we have what are now known as winter cauliflowers, or as the older generation of gardeners would have them, heading broccoli. These are sown in April and May, and are sufficiently hardy to stand the winter, heading as early as January or as late as April according to variety.

Cultivation

After germination and once the first rough leaves are in evidence the strongest looking seedlings can be pricked out into a well prepared bed 4 to 6 ins. apart in each direction, a month or so later being planted out to between 9 and 15 ins. apart with 15 to 18 ins. between rows according to variety. This results in nice bushy plants, well furnished, and with a mass of fibrous roots.

Alternatively, if such attention cannot be spared, then once their first rough leaves have developed, the plants can be transplanted directly into their permanent homes. Those selected must not have been allowed to become drawn and where possible should be leafy and short jointed.

Planting can take place at any time, but preferably on an overcast day, as seedlings can receive a severe check if allowed to stand solitarily in the burning sun. A well firmed soil is essential and if club root disease is suspected in the soil the wetting of the roots of each young plant in a jar of water followed by a dusting with calomel dust will curtail this menace.

Plant with a trowel, especially on heavy land, but the use of a dibber can be recommended on lighter soils where it will not compact the soil within the hole. Watering should be copious, especially during warm weather and until the plants are established.

A good guide as to whether they are likely to have taken is to look at them first thing in the morning when they should be stood up as straight as soldiers.

For the first few days they will probably flag badly during the day but return to the perpendicular by morning. Throughout this time watering should be continued until they stand upright all day.

The routine cultivation of all brassicas consists of regular hoeing and watching for attacks by cabbage white butterfly and cabbage whitefly. Derris or pyrethrum dust will control these pests and should be applied regularly throughout the growing season, particularly to varieties intended for autumn and winter cropping. These are in their prime during mid-summer when attacks by these pests are at their most persistent.

Sometimes odd plants in the row will turn blueish-green and will wilt, eventually dying. This will invariably have been caused by leather jackets, the larvae of the crane fly.

Uprooting the plants and probing in the surrounding soil will result in the discovery of one or two fat brownish grubs which have gorged themselves on basal stem and root effectively felling the plant.

Similar symptoms of sickness, blueish foliage and partial collapse of young plants particularly during April and May, heralds an attack by the cabbage root fly. This is not a pest which causes an odd plant in the row to die, but usually effects the whole crop. At this stage the maggots are well entrenched in the roots and surrounding soil and little can be done, however, dusting the rows of young plants a few days after transplanting with a soil insecticidal dust is a helpful preventive.

Spinach

Spinach is an excellent standby, the hardy prickly-seeded varieties being useful for sowing during summer for a late autumn picking or September for an over-wintering crop that can be harvested during early spring. Round seed spinach is a summer crop that is sown in succession little and often. Perpetual spinach or spinach beet is another old favourite. This should be sown sparingly as each seed is really a capsule containing several seeds.

They always germinate in small clumps and need careful thinning as soon as large enough to handle. Protect from sparrows in the early stages of growth using fine wire pea guards.

Strawberries and cane fruits

Of all the fruits that are available to the home gardener, strawberries and cane fruits are amongst the easiest to accommodate in a small garden. Strawberries can easily be fitted into the vegetable plot, while cane fruits can be grown along fences or walls.

Strawberries

The ideal time to establish a new strawberry bed is immediately after fruiting. Stout runners with a good strong root system can be purchased from specialist nurserymen at this time. These will be free from virus and true to name. With strawberries, never be tempted to plant runners donated by a friend as these will probably be of indeterminate variety and full of virus if taken from an established bed.

Trim the roots and remove the greater part of the foliage with a sharp knife taking care not to damage the fleshy crown. Both root-tips and old foliage invariably die when the plants are transplanted and are better removed from the beginning. Plants should be spaced at intervals of about 15 in. with 2ft. between rows or else in a double alternate row to allow for picking from both sides.

There are many varieties to choose from, but those that have the prefix Cambridge are amongst the best known and well tried.

These include Cambridge Favourite, Cambridge Rival and Cambridge Vigour.

Cultivation

Weed control is vital if a good crop of strawberries is to be produced. When the fruits start to swell and show colour it is vital to keep the soil moist. Plants should not receive excessive overhead watering as this can turn the fruits mouldy, but on the other hand spasmodic watering will lead to the development of tough unpalatable berries.

Liberal quantities of straw should be spread around the plants as the fruits develop in order to keep them clear of the ground and free of dirt and grit. A good strong net spread over the bed is also essential as birds will steal the berries immediately they start to change colour.

When fruiting is over the net should be removed straightaway to prevent plant growth becoming entangled in it. If the weather is dry when harvesting has been completed and there is no apparent danger, the straw surrounding the plants can be fired.

Blackberries and loganberries

Generally any soil will suit blackberries and loganberries but the more organic matter

Polythene protection

Strawberries can also be grown through slits in black polythene on a bed prepared by raising a 3 inch high ridge of soil.

Mat protection

The developing fruits can also be protected by placing mats around each plant rather like a collar.

that can be incorporated before planting the better. Grown against a wall or fence they are easily controlled, although many gardeners manage to train them on posts and wires across the garden without any difficulty. Irrespective of the system used, the wires will need to be spaced at 2ft. intervals and the plants grown at 10ft. centres.

After planting they should be cut down to within a few inches of the ground. New canes that are produced next season can then be tied to the wires. The following season these will bear fruit. As they complete their useful life they should be removed and young growths tied in to replace them.

Bedford Giant and Black Satin are good varieties of blackberry. The best loganberry is the thornless L654.

Raspberries

Raspberries enjoy a cool moist soil, but any that are not too dry or chalky will grow good crops. They fruit on canes which are trained on posts and wires across the garden in much the same manner as blackberries, although the raspberry's mode of growth is a little different.

The raspberry is thornless, having coarse

Clearing the bed

Cut off old leaves and unwanted runners three inches above the crowns, rake off the leaves, old straw and debris and fire it.

prickly hairs rather than vicious spines. The canes are somewhat straighter and arise as suckers that seldom yield laterals. Fruit is borne on one year old wood, the previous year's canes dying after fruiting.

Planting can take place at any time during the dormant period, newly purchased canes being cut to within a couple of feet of the ground. They should be spaced at 18 in. intervals with 5ft. between rows, wires for their subsequent growth being erected at 2ft. intervals and stretched between posts that are no more than 20ft. apart.

Routine care is much the same as for any other soft fruit, but extreme caution must be exercised when hoeing as raspberries are surface rooted plants and so are easily damaged by careless cultivation. A good mulch of well rotted manure each spring is the best cure for weeds and in addition provides nutrients and ensures constant moisture.

Old canes must be removed as soon as fruiting finishes and young growths should be tied in. Any suckers that appear between the rows can be allowed to grow to be transplanted in the autumn if extra canes are required.

Early raspberry varieties are dominated by the Malling varieties, Malling Exploit, Malling Jewel and Malling Promise. All are superficially similar, except that Malling Exploit produces the largest fruit. Malling Jewel is a trifle later flowering. Some gardeners consider it to be a mid-season variety and grow it in preference to the later Malling Enterprise. September is a good autumn fruiting kind.

Tayberries and wineberries

To add a little variety to the fruit plot try one of the more recently popularised cane fruits. Wineberries have rather small orange-red fruits, with most attractive foliage. This makes them candidates for the decorative garden as well as the fruit area. Tayberries are of a less attractive disposition, but produce large succulent fruits like enormous raspberries. Essentially fruits for the back garden, tayberries are easily grown alongside blackberries and loganberries, responding to the same cultural treatment.

Bush fruits

For the average garden bush fruits are easier to manage than tree fruits. They also give a more generous yield of fruit from a given area of land. All are hardy and crop well in the north, but with the exception of gooseberries are vulnerable to attacks by birds as the fruits are starting to ripen. A fruit cage or some kind of net covering is therefore desirable, especially for redcurrants which are otherwise decimated by blackbirds.

Planting of soft fruit takes place during the dormant period, the bushes being spaced at 4 ft centres with 5 ft between rows. Manure should be used with care, for although all soft fruit benefit from it as a mulch, when incorporated freely into the soil it encourages bush growth which is very vulnerable to mildew.

Gooseberries

There are still numerous varieties of gooseberry bushes available from nurserymen,

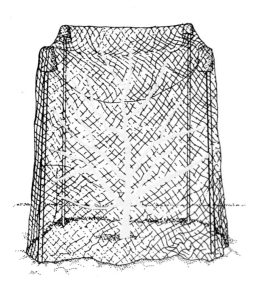

Protecting fruit

Bullfinches and sparrows take the buds from gooseberry bushes in the winter. One way to protect your fruit bushes is to grow them in a fruit cage.

despite the fact that the northern gooseberry craze has now disappeared from most places except Humberside.

In the early years of this century more than 100 varieties were available from nurserymen. These were mostly intended for showing and probably not suitable for modern needs.

The nurseryman today has the requirements of the small family garden very much in mind when selecting which varieties to grow and those that appear in his catalogue can, with one exception, be taken to be suitable for all purposes.

The odd man out is a dessert variety called Leveller, a superb gooseberry of mouth-watering succulence, but fiendishly difficult to grow to perfection.

Careless is the best variety and as its name implies is easy going. A heavy cropper, it produces medium sized greenish-yellow berries.

Keepsake is a paler fruited type and very early while Langley Gage has smallish berries that are very sweet. Lancashire Lad is the pick of the red varieties and Howard's Lancer a fine bright green kind, but this is more prone to mildew.

The pruning of gooseberries consists of keeping an open framework of branches and cutting back any longer ones that might touch the ground and root.

Most gardeners advocate the pruning of gooseberries during the autumn, but in the north where the winter weather can be harsh it is preferable to leave it until spring unless the bushes are grown in a fruit cage and protected from the birds.

Bullfinches and sparrows play havoc with the buds on gooseberry bushes in cold winter weather so if the branches are in a bit of a tangle for the winter months it acts as a deterent.

Apart from this cultivation is confined to regular weed control and a standard spraying regime with a systemic fungicide and where necessary a contact insecticide to control gooseberry sawfly.

Gooseberries are susceptible to potash deficiency in many gardens and this can be overcome by regular applications of sulphate of potash at 2oz per sq yd raked into the soil, preferably during April.

Blackcurrants

There are many varieties of blackcurrant, but amongst the most reliable for our climate are Boskoop Giant, an early kind with large berries which hang like bunches of grapes, and the mid-season Wellington XXX. This is smaller fruited and of high quality, it freezes well and makes splendid jam. Baldwin is also a very fine variety, but a temperamental character. It flourishes on some soils but performs modestly on others.

The Raven is more reliable and very similar to Baldwin, being the result of a cross between that variety and Boskoop Giant. Westwick Choice is a late sort that always does well where Wellington XXX thrives.

The blackcurrant is a most accommodating fruit which grows in almost any soil providing that it is cool and moist during summer. Being surface rooted it responds well to mulching with well rotted manure and as one of the earliest fruits to flower requires the protection of a hedge or fence to be sure that these are not damaged by frost. If natural protection cannot be provided and only a few bushes are grown, then the provision of a light covering of netting or muslin when frost is expected will be of considerable benefit.

Newly planted blackcurrant bushes should be cut down to within a couple of buds off the ground. Never be tempted to retain the wood on newly purchased bushes, for although they may realise a dish of currants the first summer the difficulty encountered when pruning the following autumn will outweigh the benefits of the few fruits harvested.

Blackcurrants fruit on year old wood which should arise from the base of the plant in order to keep it within manageable proportions. If old wood remains then the new wood will for the most part be produced as laterals from it. This makes the bush tall and unruly and it will be discovered that the length and substance of these laterals will bear no comparison to the new growths that come from the base.

Redcurrants and whitecurrants

If you cannot provide adequate protection for the fruit from birds then do not trouble about redcurrants. Whitecurrants are a little less susceptible to attack, but more often than not only because the red ones are there and seem more attractive.

As with blackcurrants, the bushes need providing with as much shelter as possible if flower damage by severe weather is to be avoided. In fact if one follows the advice given for gooseberries as regards soil conditions and treats red and whitecurrants in the same way as the black kind, then good crops should result.

The only difference is encountered when pruning for red and white varieties produce fruit on mature wood and all that is necessary is the trimming away of over-crowded or elderly branches that have finished their useful life.

Of the varieties that have been well tried in the north Red Lake and Laxtons No 1 have been reliable redcurrants, while White Versailles is the most widely planted white fruited variety.

Blueberries

If you garden on a moisture-retentive acid soil there is no reason why you should not be able to grow blueberries successfully. They are very hardy and easily grown plants which are more frequently being seen as a commercial crop. This has encouraged a number of nurseries to produce plants and these are now available to home gardeners as well.

Cultivation is confined to weed control and an occasional mulch with well rotted garden compost or pulverised bark. A high soil moisture level is vital for their success. Pruning consists of tipping back leading growths and removing any weak or weedy shoots.

In addition to their succulent fruits, blueberries have attractive small white or pinkish blossoms and foliage that often turns fiery in the autumn.

If space is restricted in the fruit area, try incorporating one or two bushes amongst other shrubs or in the mixed borders. Blueberries associate particularly well with rhododendrons and other acid-loving plants like pieris, benefiting from exactly the same kind of cultural methods.

Apples and pears

Modern rootstocks enable apples and pears to be grown in any garden or backyard. It is now quite possible to produce fruit from pot grown trees grafted on to dwarf rootstocks. Trained trees can be grown as dwarf pyramids, narrow columns or either flat espaliers or cordons. The opportunities for apple and pear cultivation have never been better.

Apples

Apples are amongst the easiest fruits to grow, even old neglected trees turning in a creditable performance. They need to be cross pollinated in order to ensure a good crop and this factor must be considered carefully when selecting suitable varieties.

The majority of apple varieties are compatible if they flower during the same period. However, if you only have room for a single tree, do not despair, for it is likely that those growing in neighbouring gardens will be quite suitable pollinators. Bees and other winged insects have no respect for garden boundaries.

Grenadier is a good early fruiting cooking variety that can be picked during August. Unfortunately it will not store and so has to be used soon after ripening. The same applies to most early kinds, those like Epicure and Worcester Pearmain not keeping for longer than two or three weeks. These can be seen in the greengrocer's to wards the end of the year, but they have been maintained in controlled storage conditions since harvest.

Mid-season varieties maturing during September and October are dominated by James Grieve, a delicious vermilion and gold, somewhat flatish fruit and the similar coloured Ellison's Orange with its distinctive sweet aniseed tang. This is the nearest in general appearance to the much loved, but temperamental, Cox's Orange Pippin.

Charles Ross is of similar aspect but larger and ready to harvest before Cox and its contemporaries, while Egremont Russet can be considered to be the King of the russets with olive-green or yellowish fruits with skin of a fine sand-papery texture.

Pears

Any garden capable of supporting a couple of fruit trees should include a pear. It used to be said that when planting pears you 'plant for your heirs', for the older pear varieties either on their own roots or grafted on seedling pear stocks did take years to come into bearing and produce a worthwhile crop. Nowadays the use of modern rootstocks means that most varieties can be dwarfed and start fruiting as quickly as apples. Two stocks are commonly used, both of approximately equal vigour. They are known as Malling A and Malling B.

These are forms of quince and are compatible with most pear varieties. However,

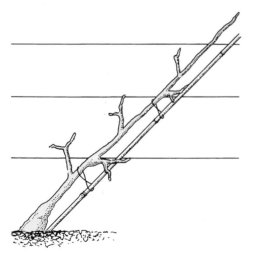
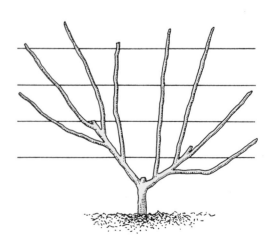

some do not take readily and have to be double-worked. This involves grafting a compatible variety onto the rootstock and allowing it to grow for a season, then grafting the incompatible desired form onto the compatible kind.

Pears, like apples, need cross pollinating. With few exceptions one variety will cross pollinate another, although the variety Bristol Cross is useless for pollination.

There are two classes of pear varieties, one which embraces those suitable for cooking and bottling and the other which we might term dessert kinds. The latter are those found listed in the nurseryman's catalogue. In most cases these can be used for cooking as well as eating raw.

Conference is undoubtedly the best known variety, a medium sized, beautifully tapered fruit of pale green with russet brown overlay. It is not ready for picking until October, but stores until well past Christmas.

William's Bon Chretien, or William's as it is more affectionately known, is also very popular and a largish pear of deep yellow with a tinge of russet and faint reddish markings. It does not keep beyond a few weeks and must be picked green during September if it is to ripen properly. Fresh pickings of Doyenne du Comice may follow, for this is not ready for harvesting until early

October. A superb variety of excellent taste and appearance which is perhaps better grown as an espalier against a wall.

Some gardeners recommend the same treatment for Winter Nelis, although it grows equally well when trained as a cordon in the open. The fruits are medium sized, somewhat rounded and greenish-yellow with a russet overlay. It is very sweet and juicy, keeping well into the New Year.

Cultivation

Growing apples and pears is largely a matter of good sense, newly planted trees being watered during dry weather and the area immediately around the trunk being kept free from weeds which may compete for nutrients in the soil. Pests and diseases should be controlled by a regular but simple spraying regime, using both a systemic insecticide and fungicide.

Pruning is the only really technical operation, and this can soon be mastered. The idea behind pruning apples and pears is to build a strong framework in a young tree and control growth so that the maximum number of fruiting spurs or shoots are produced evenly along its branches. The removal of suckers from the base of the tree is also very important in conserving the tree's energy.

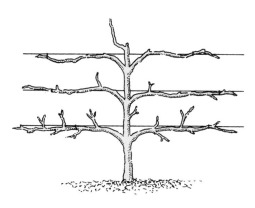

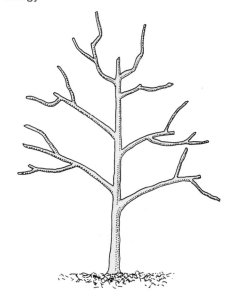

Training fruit trees

It is now possible to produce fruit from pot grown trees grafted on to dwarf rootstocks. Trained trees can be grown as, from left, cordon, fan, espalier and pyramid.

Plums, cherries and peaches

The stone fruits are very useful garden trees, for all produce most attractive spring blossom as well as fruits. You may not think that you have room for the luxury of such fruit, but when their dual purpose value is taken into account, then a purely decorative tree can often justifiably be substituted with a plum, cherry, peach or other stone fruit.

Plums

Many plum varieties struggle under northern conditions, so it is useful to see what is growing well locally and then from amongst these varieties choose what you find most palatable.

Selecting the variety to grow is also dependant to a certain extent upon the amount of space available. If only one can be grown, then a self-fertile variety must be chosen, but where several can be accommodated or a neighbour has a tree or two well established then there is more freedom of choice.

If sterile or partially self-fertile varieties are desired, then care should be taken to ensure that they flower at the same time. Early flowering kinds have no chance of pollinating late flowering varieties. It is also important to plant the earlier varieties in a sheltered part of the garden to give as much protection from frost as possible.

Some growers classify plums as cooking or dessert, and while a number of kinds are excellent for eating fresh, those that are normally recommended for cooking make good eating when thoroughly ripe.

Victoria is the best of the utility kinds, a gorgeous red plum. Being self-fertile, it can be grown alone. Czar is a deep mauve-blue self-fertile sort which yields regular heavy crops. Its fruits are perhaps not up to the standard of Coe's Golden Drop, but then this is handicapped by being self-sterile.

Greengages are plums too. Oullin's Golden Gage is the finest. An early fruiting kind that needs to be established for a year or two before coming into bearing. Early Transparent Gage is not of such good quality, but is a regular cropper and like Oullin's Golden Gage is self-fertile.

Giant Prune is a fascinating plum of a deep reddish colour borne on a vigorous tree with stout upright branches. The damson types are also handy, being the best kind of plum for converting into jam.

Plums are gross feeders and when grown in the open benefit from liberal quantities of well rotted manure or garden compost applied as a mulch. When planted against a wall a certain amount of caution should be exercised otherwise they will become too vigorous. It is important to use the manure as a mulch and not fork it in, or indeed perform anything much in the way of surface cultivation as damaging the roots will encourage the proliferation of suckers.

Pruning consists mainly of tidying up the trees and is best performed in spring just before bud-break. This restricts the entry of silver leaf disease which often manifests itself on trees pruned at the onset of winter. Trees trained against a wall may need considerable thinning during summer to keep them in order.

Cherries

There is a question mark over the viability of cherries in the small garden, although in recent times dwarf varieties like the dark red fruited Cherokee, which is also self-pollinating, has made doubtful gardeners consider them again seriously. To yield satisfactory crops traditional cherry varieties need to be grown as standard trees and allowed plenty of space. Those splendid eating cherries Merton Heart, Bigarreau Napoleon and Early Rivers all need cross pollinating and masses of space in which to develop.

Of traditional cherries the cooking variety Morello is most useful to the home gardener. This is self-fertile and productive when fan trained. Cherries fruit on the previous season's growth, so older branches should be periodically reduced in order to encourage replacement of young shoots.

Peaches, nectarines and apricots

Although they are regarded as fruits from warmer climates, there is no reason why, with a little care, these should not be successful in the north. The trees are perfectly hardy, it is just that they blossom when frost damage is likely.

Obviously the only way to guarantee a regular crop is to go for glasshouse cultivation. However, the disadvantage of this is that the trees, even when trained against the wall or in the roof, take up a lot of space and cast considerable shade to the detriment of crops below.

Outdoors they are best grown on the fan system against a sheltered wall, for then when frost threatens a fine net can be draped over them to give some measure of protection. Likewise when the fruit is ripening a rather coarser net can be used to keep blackbirds at bay.

Peach varieties are abundant, Amsden June being the earliest and ripening in July, while the large and handsome Duke of York is only a week or two later. Peregrine is a medium sized fruit of excellent quality that is ready in early August. If you are prepared to risk it you can extend the season until the end of September by planting Prince of Wales.

Nectarines are a sort of smooth skinned peach and are not quite so popular. Although numerous varieties have been developed, only the July cropping Early Rivers and the extremely fine August ripening kind Lord Napier are commonly available.

The number of varieties of apricot available to the home gardener are not large and dominated by Moorpark, a large, rounded, yellowish fruit with one side of a reddish-brown colour. This is seldom ripe before early September.

The cultivation of apricots, peaches and nectarines is broadly similar, the difference in habit being that the apricot bears fruit on spurs as well as on young wood. This means that when pruning, unwanted lateral shoots should be cut back to two buds instead of being removed altogether.

Apricot fruits scarcely need thinning, whereas peaches and nectarines need to be left four or five inches apart. Otherwise treatment is the same, all three kinds enjoying warm sunny conditions preferably on an alkaline soil.

1 Pinching shoots

The growing points of unwanted shoots of peaches, apricots and nectarines should be pinched back.

2 Thinning fruit

Peaches and nectarines should be left four or five inches apart by pinching out the fruit when they are the size of a large pea.

Other fruit, vegetables and nuts

Amongst our popular fruiting garden plants are a number that do not neatly fit into any particular compartment. More often than not they are confined to a corner of the garden or else become part of the decorative area.

Rhubarb

Whether rhubarb is a fruit or vegetable is questionable. It is very popular for forcing and securing an early crop. This kind of cultivation demands that the crowns are at least three years old, those that are intended for forcing being lifted and allowed to lie on the surface of the soil to be frosted. This pre-chilling is necessary for speedy forcing.

After two or three weeks of frosting and weathering the crowns are taken inside. Rhubarb can be successfully forced in the garage or garden shed, under the greenhouse staging or even in the open ground with the aid of a bucket or an old chimney pot.

Watering during the forcing period is very important. While the crowns should be kept damp, they should never be wet, for not only does this encourage fungal diseases, but it spoils the quality and colour of the stalks.

Initially the forcing temperature should not exceed 45F, however, when there is a possibility of gradually raising the temperature to 55F after ten days, the crop will be ready about two weeks sooner.

Forcing crowns in the open using an old bucket or chimney pot is a little more difficult as the temperature cannot be controlled, so obviously the crop takes longer to come to maturity. Nevertheless it is still worth doing if you do not have a suitable indoor facility.

Asparagus

Asparagus is an easy perennial vegetable crop to grow. Plant in well prepared soil during April. Each crown is like a small octopus and should just be covered with soil. Do not harvest spears the first season. Keep the bed clear of weeds. A crop can be taken the second year, sufficient fern being allowed to remain to ensure that a good crop ensues the following season.

Nuts

There are innumerable kinds of nuts, varying from the sweet chestnut and walnut to the tiny beech nut, but only the cob nuts and filberts are worth considering in the small garden. The cob nut is the type in which the outer husk is very short, while the filbert has a long outer husk which totally enfolds it.

Nuts will grow in most soils, but a free-draining loam is ideal. Unlike other fruiting plants nuts produce catkins in both male and female forms which are pollinated by the wind. These appear during February and March, and once their work is done the bushes can be pruned, enough nut-bearing wood being left to give a reasonable crop. Wood that carried a crop the previous year must also be spurred back.

Walnuts and sweet chestnuts are for larger gardens only. They are large trees with an extensive spreading canopy. If you have room incorporate them into the general garden scene, perhaps as a single lawn specimen. Both are ideal for growing in grass which provides a soft landing for the fruits. The sweet chestnut is unlikely to produce quality nuts except in an exceptionally hot season. The walnut will, although it may take twenty years before it starts.

Medlar

The medlar is a traditional fruit of Victorian fruit gardens, but it is also a most attractive tree. With apple-like foliage and large white blossoms it is well suited to the decorative garden, especially one of an informal nature. The strange fruits, which look rather like enlarged rose hips but of a brownish hue, are picked just before ripening and then spread out in trays, not being used until they begin to decompose. This ripening process is known as bletting.

Quince

Like the medlar, to which it is closely related, the quince is a fine ornamental tree. Cultivation is the same as for the medlar except that the fruits are used when ripe and should not be picked until they are fully mature.

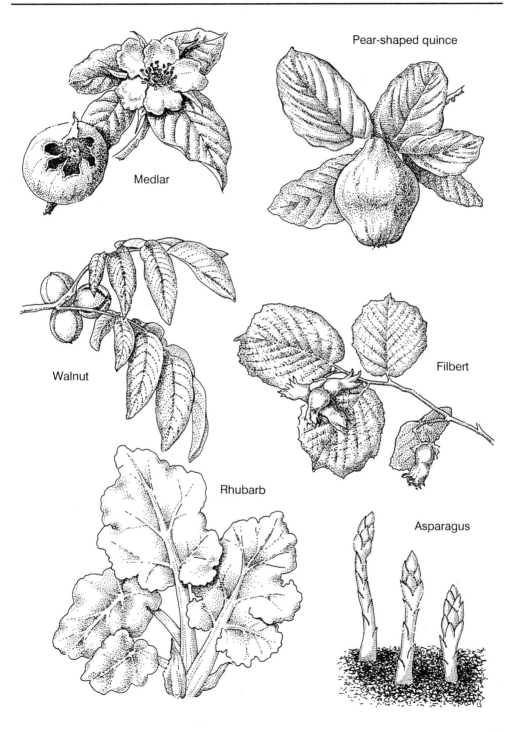

Medlar

Pear-shaped quince

Walnut

Filbert

Rhubarb

Asparagus

Greenhouse and frame

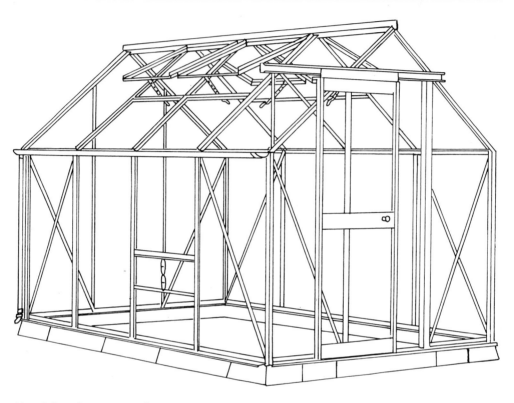

Aluminium frame greenhouse
Span roof type. Note the side and ridge ventilation and the wide door for easy access.

Greenhouse styles

Greenhouses are available in all manner of shapes and sizes and take forms that vary from the conservatory and sun lounge to the enclosed porch around the front door. All are very useful and can accommodate a surprisingly large number of plants.

Modern greenhouses basically come in four forms; the lean-to, in which one wall is formed by the dwelling house or other substantial building; the span roof type, which is built on a dwarf wall and has a pitched roof; the Dutch light kind, formerly constructed on Dutch lights but in the modern form glass to ground greenhouse, and the hexagonal type that is, broadly speaking, dome-shaped but with angular sides. All

have their advocates, but it is generally conceded that the span roof type proves to be the most versatile when a wide range of plants are to be grown.

Greenhouse construction

Greenhouses can be constructed of many different materials. Polythene houses are cheap to purchase initially, but need re-covering every two years and in winter will often suffer wind or snow damage.

Those made from corrugated perspex are little better, cracking and discolouring with the weather, although polycarbonate can be recommended. Glass is obviously the most satisfactory material to use, but the most suitable material for the framework is more difficult to decide. Cedar and teak that are kept well oiled are obviously ideal, but extremely expensive, while ordinary softwood painted in white looks good but has a very limited life.

Aluminium would seem to be the best answer as it does not rust, but with some glasshouses the bolts and screws holding them together are made from steel and are liable to corrode. So inspect any intended purchase of this kind very carefully.

Ideally staging should be provided at waist height down either side and a shelf near the ridge is handy if this can be kept above head height. Ventilation must be adequate and most gardeners agree that both side and ridge ventilators are essential during the summer months.

A good wide door is necessary for easy management. It should be wide enough to take a wheel-barrow without skinning your fingers and with no tiresome step or ramp.

Heating

Heating is desirable, but may be prohibitively expensive. If you do decide to heat your greenhouse then purchase an electrical fan type.

Not only does this provide warmth, but it also circulates the air on muggy days in autumn. In the summer the fan can be switched to the cool air position to reduce the high temperatures.

Gas and paraffin heaters are not so desirable as they produce a damp heat, and by virtue of their mode of operation do not readily circulate the air.

Insulating

If you are able to afford to heat your greenhouse, it also makes sense to insulate it to minimise heat loss. There are many methods of doing this, but the clear plastic bubble insulation material now available is simple to fix and rarely causes any problems with condensation.

Clear polythene has always been considered to be the most suitable insulation, causing minimal reduction in light and trapping a barrier of air between. It has always been associated with condensation, a build up of light-reducing algae, and a fragility which is not so evident in modern clear bubble insulation.

Whether you go for this or traditional polythene, it is important when fastening it to the internal structure of the greenhouse that provision is made for the opening of ventilators.

Insulation may well still be useful at night during spring, but on sunny days the temperature will rocket and full ventilation may be necessary.

If you cannot afford to heat your greenhouse, then consider investing in either a small propagator or a heated bench. Both are very useful and give the facility much greater versatility.

Siting

Correct siting of the greenhouse is vital if plants are to develop properly. Choose an open part of the garden in full sun. It is a simple matter to shade a modern small greenhouse if the sun becomes too bright. The uncontrollable shade of a tree or building can lead to very poor growth.

The garden frame

A garden frame is as invaluable as a greenhouse in its own way. The fact that you have a greenhouse does not mean a frame is unnecessary. In many ways it is essential as it provides the half-way house between greenhouse and open ground, enabling plants to be hardened off gently before being planted out.

There are nearly as many designs for frames as there are for greenhouses, and while the traditional Dutch light type is still the most useful, the modern pitched roof kind has much to commend it.

Frames can be permanent with a dwarf brick wall and floor of concrete or gravel, or else of bottomless structure to enable them to be moved on to the soil in any part of the garden. Even the use of a deep box with a sheet of glass over it is a variation of a frame and quite startling results can be achieved with such a simple device.

Greenhouse management

The successful management of a greenhouse depends upon following simple rules regularly and applying common sense. A greenhouse is a responsibility rather like a dog or cat, for no day goes by without its inhabitants demanding some attention.

Watering

Regular watering may seem obvious, but it is surprising how many gardeners water when they have to, to the detriment of the plants. Good stable growth can never be achieved by irregular watering.

A humid atmosphere is beneficial, especially during the summer months. Regular spraying of the path and gravel under the benches helps. Avoid getting water on the foliage of plants during hot sunny weather. The droplets of water serve as small magnifying glasses during bright weather and the tissue beneath becomes scorched. During the late spring and peak summer period the greenhouse must be provided with some kind of shading. Roller blinds are expensive, but good, although most of the sun shade products that are mixed with water and applied with a brush are equally functional, if not as visually pleasing.

Ventilation

Ventilation should be applied freely during warm weather and moderately during cooler periods. The free circulation of air amongst plants helps to reduce the incidence of fungal diseases like botrytis.

During the duller days of winter and early spring ensure that maximum light is admitted to the greenhouse. Clean the glass in the autumn and then again during early spring. Cleanliness is important in all parts of the structure if pests and diseases are to be successfully controlled.

The thorough cleansing of rafters, brickwork and other fixtures during the winter with a solution of potassium permanganate and water, or a heavy disinfectant like Jeyes Fluid will pay dividends.

Dead leaves and discarded plants should be disposed of regularly and should

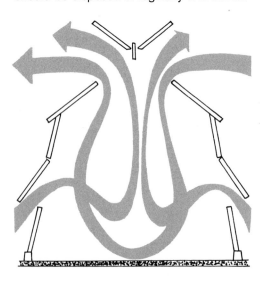

1 Shading

Sunshade products applied with a brush work just as well as expensive roller blinds.

2 Ventilation

Free circulation of air amongst plants helps reduce the incidence of fungal diseases.

not be allowed to accumulate beneath the staging where they will harbour pests and diseases. Regular cleaning and maintenance results in healthy plants and a trouble-free structure in which to produce them.

Repotting

One of the on-going activities in a well managed greenhouse is repotting. This applies to all permanent plants and those that are growing on and need periodic removal to a larger pot size. Some flowering plants like pot chrysanthemums and primulas are completely exhausted after flowering and are best discarded rather than re-potted. They rarely regain their former glory.

Repotting often causes some consternation, particularly to new gardeners, for there is believed to be a certain mystique surrounding the operation and an uncertainty as to when to perform it. It is obviously better to repot a plant just before it needs it, but the newcomer may have difficulty in recognising just when that is, so plants are often allowed to go beyond that point and start to deteriorate.

Paleness of foliage and gaunt appearance is the overall aspect of a plant that is in need of repotting. The potball will be hard and congested, often with roots pushing out through the drainage holes of the pot. The compost surface will also probably have a stale look about it heightened by the presence of mosses or liverworts.

When repotted, pot-bound plants rapidly recover from their ordeal but it is better to catch them before they go into decline so that strong healthy growth can continue unchecked. During the active growing period do not be frightened to turn a plant out of its pot and inspect the rootball. There is no need to pull it about, but a regular inspection will indicate whether everything is in good order.

Do not pay too much regard to the concentrated presence of roots towards the sides of the pot, for it is quite natural for them to gravitate there. It is not necessarily an indication that the plant must be repotted. Similarly roots that push through the drainage holes may not always indicate congestion within the pot, for if the pot has been stood on a gravel tray in moist conditions it is quite normal for roots to probe around outside.

The best way to tell whether a plant needs repotting is to pinch the rootball with your fingers. If there is any give in the compost it shows that the potball has not been completely ramified by roots and therefore nothing need yet be done. If the rootball feels hard and solid, then repotting is clearly a matter of priority. Repotting is also necessary if you spot tiny flies jumping around on the surface of the compost. These are feeding on decomposing organic matter in a compost that has passed its useful life. They disappear immediately after repotting.

Feeding

Most greenhouse plants need feeding if they are to give of their best. This is most effective when they are in active growth, either immediately after they have started to sprout or following the formation of flower buds. The feeding regime is different for individual plant types, but the exact rates that should be used will be found on the containers of modern proprietory plant foods. The levels of nitrate, phosphate and potash are also noted, so that a suitable feed can be chosen depending upon whether it is to be directed to fruit and flower production or foliage and root.

Spraying

It is important to introduce a general spraying regime to the glasshouse. Irrespective of the plants being grown, insect pests and fungal diseases will appear. Check carefully that the fungicide and insecticide mix so that you can spray in one go. Instructions will be clearly stated on the package. These will also indicate plant sensitivity.

Systemic pesticides are the only ones that can be used for such a spraying programme. These are absorbed by the foliage, taken into the sap stream of the plant and serve as an innoculation. To maintain the protection, spraying will be required every three weeks or so.

There are certain pests and diseases that are not controlled effectively by systemics and these need dealing with individually with contact pesticides.

Fruit and vegetables under glass

There are innumerable fruits and vegetables which can be grown successfully in the average domestic greenhouse. Not all will successfully co-exist and care needs to be taken, particularly with vines, to ensure that they do not exclude too much light to the detriment of other plants.

Cucumbers

There are several different ways of growing cucumbers, but most gardeners prefer to use grow bags. It is unwise to cultivate cucumbers in pots as this is too restricting. The cucumber is a vine-like plant which should be trained on wires in the roof of the greenhouse. A short cane should be placed next to each plant long enough to reach the lowest of the overhead wires.

The plants are lightly fastened to the wires, care being taken not to damage the foliage. Sideshoots are produced from every leaf joint, but none below the first wire should be allowed to develop. When the lower wire is reached the plant can be trained as high into the roof as required and then stopped, any side branches being spread out on each side.

Most of these will produce flowers, the female ones having a tiny cucumber behind them, the male ones on a short thin stem. The male flowers should be immediately removed to prevent pollination. If fertilisation takes place, the fruits, instead of growing straight and slim, will become club-shaped, full of seed and very bitter.

Once the embyro fruit have formed, the side branches or laterals should be pinched out at two leaves past the last fruit to prevent further growth. This will also hasten fruit development.

Tomatoes

Most gardeners use grow bags for tomatoes too. They are planted into the bags by carefully puncturing the polythene at intervals and planting through the holes. The tomatoes are then in a rich growing medium with what is in effect a polythene mulch.

Once growing strongly, tomatoes should be staked or strung to the greenhouse roof.

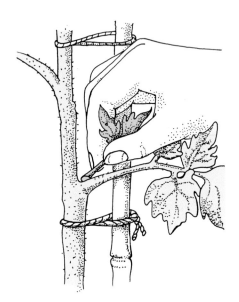

1 Pinching out

Remove side shoots from tomatoes as they appear.

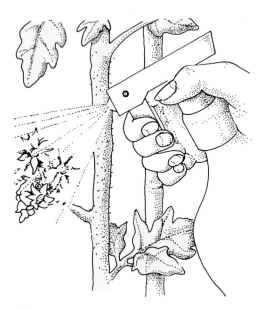

2 Spraying

Syringe the open flowers with tepid water to aid the setting of fruit. The plants themselves must also be kept well watered.

The plants should be allowed to develop until about eight trusses or clusters of flowers have formed. The growing point must then be removed. As growth progresses all the shoots that appear in the axils of the leaves must be pinched out. Leaving them produces an unruly plant that is difficult to control and reduces the quality of the fruit.

The open flowers which are produced in regularly placed trusses are small and a greenish-yellow colour. They should be syringed with tepid water regularly to aid the setting of fruit. The plants themselves must be kept well watered and once the fruits are forming a liquid tomato fertilizer should be administered at ten day intervals.

As the fruits swell and ripen, the older lower leaves, which by then will be turning brownish or yellow, can be removed to admit light and allow for the free circulation of air. Do not remove a lot of fresh green foliage as this is assisting in the development of both plant and fruit.

Grapevines

Grapevines are gross feeders, so if you plan to plant one in the greenhouse border, be aware that it will compete heavily with adjacent plants for nutrients. This is why traditionally grapes have been planted in the soil outside the greenhouse, the rod or stem being trained through a hole in the wall. For the first couple of years after planting a vine it should not be allowed to fruit, the leading growth being cut back by about half every December and the laterals stopped at two sound buds. In February the rods must be removed from their support and bent down to encourage even bud break. Once growth starts they are tied back in position.

The third year after planting a small crop can be taken, the laterals carrying the bunches being stopped at two leaves beyond the last bunch and all other growths pinched back to one leaf. The tendrils may also be removed.

As soon as the tiny fruits have formed and have a good hold on life they must be thinned with scissors so that the individual grapes remain an inch or so apart.

It is important to keep the roots of vines moist at all times, many gardeners flood them just before flowering and again after thinning. Shading should be given when necessary and adequate ventilation provided to prevent the fruit going mouldy before they ripen.

There are a multitude of varieties to choose from, the white fruited Muscat of Alexandria and the well known Black Hamburg both being reliable for unheated greenhouses here in the north.

Down-to-earth tip

When preparing a grow bag for planting do not overlook the means of support for the plants. Strings and canes that can easily be used with a plant growing in a pot or border are more difficult to deal with in a growing bag. Before planting, push the growing bag between the gaps in several wire coat hangers. One for each plant. Position them next to the planting hole. The hooked part of the hanger is perfect for fastening a string to and taking up into the roof of the greenhouse.

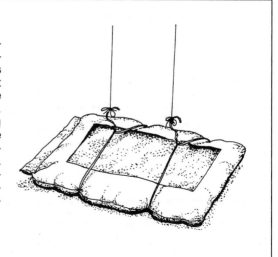

The mixed greenhouse

The majority of gardeners have to operate a mixed greenhouse – one where flowers, fruit and vegetables are grown together. This is not ideal, for rarely can any one crop be grown to perfection. However, most can be raised very satisfactorily. The methods by which those such as tomatoes, cucumbers and grapes can be grown are described on pages 96 and 97.

Temperate plants

When a greenhouse is used for all kinds of plants it is usual to have some kind of structural planting or special plants in containers to form a backbone. As many home gardeners can only afford to keep the temperature in the greenhouse just above freezing the temperate plants from the Mediterranean and Australasia that are best employed.

The most familiar and desirable is the yellow florists' mimosa or acacia, an aimiable fellow with finely divided fern-like foliage and myriad fragrant fluffy blossoms produced during January and February. It is the hardiest acacia and can sometimes be found growing successfully outdoors in southern England.

Acacia longifolia has a similar reputation for hardiness and will certainly tolerate two or three degrees of frost. With its slender lance-shaped foliage and bright tufted spikes of brilliant yellow blossoms it enjoys life in the sun room.

The blackwood acacia is a similar proposition and well worth growing but the most remarkable of this family is the cootamundra wattle. This will form a sizeable shrub if left to its own devices, although it responds well to careful pruning, rewarding the gardener with an absolute mass of bright yellow flowers during the dark and dreary days of winter.

Albizzias are near relatives of the acacias and have finely divided foliage and fluffy flowers of pink, reddish, or occasionally a light sulphurous hue. Some are hardy when planted against a south or west facing wall, but most are reliable as pot plants.

The commonest kind is known as the julibrissin. This is rather like a mimosa but with pink blossoms. It is a most fascinating plant, for at the approach of evening it collapses completely, the foliage and young branches hanging limply until dawn breaks the following day.

Australian lilac or hardenbergia is another member of the pea family worth more than a second glance. A scrambling twining plant with almost evergreen foliage and striking lavender-purple blossoms, it is ideal for training on a framework, or better still into the greenhouse roof.

No collection of temperate plants is complete without the clianthus or New Zealand lobster claw. A shrubby or scrambling plant, it produces the most magnificent scarlet claw-like flowers amongst finely divided grey-green foliage. One of the most spectacular plants for the unheated greenhouse.

Winter colour

Many gardeners use their greenhouse for growing tomatoes and cucumbers during the summer and perhaps raising a few bedding plants in the spring. When late summer comes and the crops are coming to an end, the old growing bags are removed, the greenhouse cleaned and then used as a store for the wheelbarrow or bicycle. This is a shame, for with a little effort and the selection of suitable plants it can be transformed for the winter into an alpine house.

There is no particular greenhouse that is better than any other for such a project, although alpine specialists do make adaptations to allow for more ventilation. Adequate light is of course vital and most gardeners agree that the span-roofed kind of structure is the easiest to manage.

Alpine plants require no artificial heat, the only occasion when a fan heater on low heat might be useful is for dispersing the moisture-laden air on a damp foggy morning. It should never be used for raising the temperature and promoting growth.

Alpine plants are usually grown in pans and displayed around the greenhouse on staging, although some enthusiasts bed the pans in a gritty medium to create a more natural effect. While this may look very good, it is also very heavy, and before attempting such an undertaking the staging should be strengthened considerably.

The cultivation of alpines under glass is not at all complicated providing that you always give maximum light and ventilation. Be careful over the selection of compost too, for alpines require a free-draining gritty medium if they are to prosper. Except for the lime-haters, John Innes Potting Compost No 2 with about a quarter by volume of sharp grit added is a good general medium.

When choosing alpine plants for the winter greenhouse avoid the more boisterous kinds like white arabis and yellow alyssum. However, the greenhouse need not just be the preserve of the rare or unusual, nor only those that require a dry and cool environment. Much enjoyment can be derived from growing ordinary well behaved alpines to greater perfection than is possible under outdoor conditions on the rock garden.

A misconception amongst many gardeners is that the alpine house is only useful and colourful during spring. While it is true that it looks at its best between February and April, colour and fragrance can be provided throughout the year with careful planning if you wish.

Dwarf bulbs are particularly useful for the permanent alpine display, for there are species and varieties that will provide colour for most of the year, although spring and autumn are obviously the peak seasons. Small shrubby and herbaceous plants also make a contribution, for such a greenhouse is a haven for all that is choice and interesting in the alpine world.

It is not uncommon for a gardener who starts with a mixed greenhouse growing tomatoes and cucumbers during the summer and alpines during winter and early spring to switch entirely to alpines and buy his tomatoes and cucumbers from the greengrocer! This form of greenhouse gardening can be addictive and is particularly useful for the elderly or less able as it is virtually devoid of heavy lifting.

Greenhouse innovations

The mixed greenhouse lends itself to the introduction of a number of modern innovations. Indeed, it is desirable from a maintenance point of view to take advantage of any labour saving devices that are available.

Watering has traditionally been managed by hand using a watering can. With a mixed collection of plants, other than alpines, it can become more or less automated. A simple capillary system with a small feeder tank fitted with a ball-cock can save hours and ensure that in brief periods of absence the plants are kept moist.

A feeder is taken to a capillary mat, which is placed upon the staging, and the pots are stood on this. Providing that the compost is moist and firm contact is made between the base of the pot and the mat, water will travel by capillary attraction. The main requirement for this system of watering is level staging. It is not a complicated system to install and is widely available in do-it-yourself kit form.

Ventilation can be automated by simple automatic vent openers. These are now very accurate and ensure a desirable flow of air through the greenhouse. Such openers do not require any connection to electricity and function totally independently. A boon during early spring when bright sunshine can suddenly raise the temperature too high.

Pest control is more difficult in a greenhouse with a mixture of plants. Instead of spraying individuals and being concerned about whether the spray is compatible with the plants, invest in some of the sticky plastic insect strips. These are very efficient, although they tend not to discriminate between helpful and troublesome insects.

Capillary bench

An uncomplicated system for automated watering which is available in DIY kit form.

Conservatory and house plants

The conservatory or sun lounge is becoming a very important part of the modern home. It is a place to sit and relax away from our often inclement weather and also is an ideal situation in which to grow a wide variety of plants. If you do not aspire to such elegance, then the chances are that you will have a window ledge or two on which half hardy and tropical plants can be grown successfully.

The conservatory

The Victorians, who were largely responsible for introducing and popularising the conservatory, had very labour intensive displays of plants. We should not be trying to recreate these.

With modern varieties of plants the decorative aspect can exist alongside relaxation for we now have available a finer range of robust and easily cultivated indoor plants than the Victorians could have imagined.

Plants for low temperatures and of compact habit are widely available. Along with their increased resistance to diseases and the ready availability of easily administered and safe pesticides a display of equal merit to anything seen last century is possible for much less expense and effort.

Choose easy-going foliage subjects like yuccas and palms. These mostly tolerate a varying temperature regime and can put up with a degree of irregular watering. Oleanders and umbrella plants are also resilient, so too are some of the fruiting plants such as fig and avocado, although the latter is unlikely to produce fruits in the average conservatory. These structural plants form the backbone of the display, seasonal subjects like spring and summer flowering bulbs, together with annual flowers such as schizanthus, salpiglossis, browallia and primulas providing highlights of easily managed colour.

The window ledge

The greatest obstacle to the successful cultivation of house plants is presented by central heating. The air is so dry that the plants suffer. Only spiny cacti and fleshy succulents really enjoy the conditions of the modern home. The effect of dryness can be overcome quite simply by creating a microclimate around every plant. Plunge each pot in a larger pot or bowl and fill the extra space with peat that is kept continually moist. The dampness rising from the peat will create sufficient humidity to keep most plants happy.

Although the majority of house plants appreciate moist air, they do not need too much water, especially during the winter months. Over-watering is the commonest reason for house plants failing. Dampness is all that is required, the surface of the compost being moist to the touch but not exuding water if gently pressed with the fingers.

Some plants like Christmas azaleas are usually grown in clay pots. A good indication as to the necessity for watering is to tap the pot with a small length of wood. If a dull thud is emitted then it is quite wet enough, but if the pot makes a ringing sound it needs some attention. The higher the ringing note, the drier the plant.

When a plant has obviously been over-watered and its leaves are limp and yellowing, it can often be revived by re-potting. Knock it out of its pot and shake off as much of the wet compost as possible without damaging the roots, replacing it in fresh compost in the same pot.

Draughts and fluctuating temperatures are second only to over-watering as a cause of house plant loss. The leaves of affected plants turning limp and yellowish and often becoming brown and parchment-like around the edges. Shutting the plants behind the curtains is the most usual reason for this malady, for it is seldom appreciated that the temperature drop once the curtains are drawn is both sudden and prolonged.

That is not to say that house plants should be kept out of the window. On the contrary, during autumn and winter all plants need as much light as they can get. It is desirable to turn each pot regularly. This ensures even foliage development resulting in a shapely plant which is not so likely to drop its foliage prematurely. Leaves on the room side of a plant grown on a window ledge have a much shorter life than those provided with as much light as possible. A quarter turn of the pot daily is sufficient.

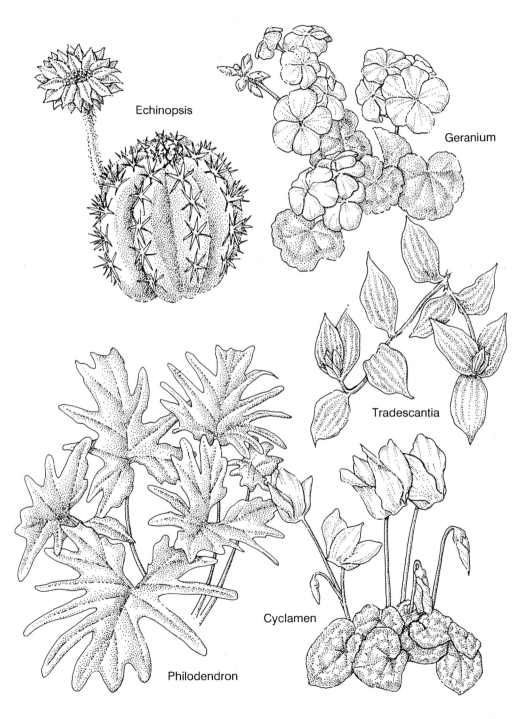

Echinopsis

Geranium

Tradescantia

Cyclamen

Philodendron

Weed control

The control of weeds is fundamental to good garden management. Weeds not only look untidy, but rob neighbouring plants of nutrients, play host to pests and diseases and shade out desirable subjects resulting in their sickly, weak growth. Handweeding is often necessary in the immediate vicinity of plants, although with care a hoe can often be used to good effect.

In formal parts of the garden, like the vegetable plot, the hoe is the most efficient method of weed control, not only destroying the weeds before they have a chance to get a hold, but also creating a well aired surface tilth of soil.

Weed control

Although weedkillers often have a reputation for being toxic and unpleasant; this does not apply to all of them. Even the residual kinds are nowadays much more environmentally friendly than the sodium chlorate of yesteryear. On paths and other areas where it is not intended to grow plants, these provide protection for up to 18 months. There are a number of systemic herbicides, but most contain glyphosate as the active ingredient. It is these that should always be used by the home gardener. Glyphosate is especially useful as it is inactivated when it falls upon the soil. It only reacts to green foliage. It is important that the weeds are growing vigorously before it is applied. The more luxuriant the weed growth, the more rapid the kill, although do not expect overnight success. The method of translocation by which such a weedkiller works means that it may be two or three weeks before results are evident.

Although this method of weed control is efficient, any contact that the weedkiller makes with garden plants will be fatal. Systemic weedkillers are not selective in their action, so that any that gets sprayed on to the foliage of other green plants like shrubs or roses will just as readily cause their demise. However, it is this kind of garden chemical which has revolutionised our gardening, making it both efficient and very safe.

Unlike some of the weedkillers of the past, those containing glyphosate do not cause horrific burning disfigurement of weeds. They work from inside, causing extensive disruption of the growing points and eventual collapse.

This means that it is not a poison in the sense that it is toxic if children play in sprayed areas. It is a matter of common sense to allow the spray to dry on the foliage so that it can be absorbed properly, but there is no reason why pets or children should not run and play amongst sprayed grass or weed areas later the same day.

1 Handweeding

This is often necessary close to plants.

2 Polythene mulching

Particularly useful in the vegetable plot.

3 Hoeing

The most efficient weed control in the formal garden.

Wildlife is unlikely to be disturbed, except eventually by the lack of leafy cover, but if the area is being replanted soon afterwards with garden plants, then the species mix is likely to enrich the area with wildlife rather than deplete it.

The fact that the soil can be cultivated and planted immediately afterwards is a great bonus but it is important that perennials are allowed at least seven days to absorb the weedkiller.

Contact weedkillers based on paraquat are very efficient for annual weeds, but they must be used with great respect. They have little lasting effect on perennial weeds, merely burning off the foliage. Leaves are quickly replaced, but the weeds are obviously weakened by the experience. Such weedkillers depend upon destroying the plant tissue on to which they fall and so complete spray cover of the foliage is necessary if there is to be a reasonable kill.

Following the chemical killing of weeds amongst woody plants like shrubs and roses subsequent weed control can be es-

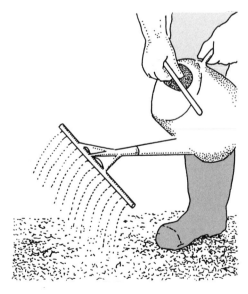

4 Spraying
Using a spray bar. Weedkillers must be used and stored with respect.

tablished by the liberal use of mulching materials. Not only do these suppress weeds, but they conserve moisture as well. Well rotted manure or garden compost are excellent weed suppressors, but composted bark should be treated with caution. If the bark has not been properly composted it deprives the soil of nitrogen as it decomposes, yellowing foliage on established plantings.

Some gardeners use black polythene or fabric mulches. These are effective, but have limitations. They are most easily used in the vegegtable garden or amongst fruit bushes which are growing in formal rows. The plants are planted through slits cut in the polythene or fabric at the appropriate distances. The material excludes light and prevents seedling weeds from growing. Moisture still percolates beneath the mulch, the material itself preventing a considerable soil moisture loss. It is an ugly method of weed suppression, but in the ordered vegetable patch can be tolerated. In the decorative garden such mulches are sometimes used for permanent features like conifer beds. In such circumstances the mulch is generally disguised by a generous covering of chippings.

However, mulching is not a proposition for other garden features like the rock garden. Established plants resent it. The only method of chemical weed control here is a herbicidal touch weeder. This is an impregnated stick of weedkiller with which you can dab offending weeds. Otherwise it must be hand weeding.

Storing weedkillers

The storage of weedkillers, and indeed any other garden chemicals, must be taken seriously. Always lock them all away safely out of the reach of children. It is important that they are kept in a cool dry place and that you maintain a separate list of what you have in store. If you decide to use paraquat or any similar quick acting but dangerous herbicide, be sure to have a regulation cover-all suit. It is of great benefit when spraying anywhere and with all kind of garden chemicals it is certainly better to be safe than sorry.

103

Pests and diseases outdoors

Few plants are immune from the predations of pests and diseases, but much can be achieved in their control by good garden hygiene. Do not allow piles of fallen leaves to build up or other garden debris and weeds to accumulate. Apart from providing a haven for pests and diseases, weeds often serve as a host in their life cycle.

Pests

Slugs and snails are unquestionably the greatest pests in the garden. They chew the foliage of seedlings and adult plants with equal impunity. Some slugs live underground and eat holes in potatoes, carrots and other root crops. These are small slugs called keel slugs and are extremely difficult to control.

Scrupulous hygiene which denies them places in which to hide goes a long way to providing a control. Populations of slugs that live in the soil can be destroyed by turning the soil up during the winter and allowing it to be frosted. This will not effect a complete eradication, but it will make a significant difference.

Slug pellets and liquids used sparingly and in areas of great slug and snail activity can make great reductions in the population, but some gardeners do not like to use these chemicals for the fear of birds picking up tainted corpses. Where this is seen as a problem, slugs and snails can be easily captured by taking the eaten halves of grapefruit and inverting them on the soil. Leave them overnight and in the morning they will be full of the pests. You can dispose of them as you see fit.

Caterpillars, especially of butterflies like the cabbage white, can cause devastation to plants, leaving the leaves skeletonised. Sawfly caterpillars and those of the winter moth are also extremely damaging to a wide range of plants.

Systemic insecticides are not so effective against caterpillars. Their control depends upon contact killers such as pyrethrum or derris. Use the powder form and dust the plants liberally.

Vine weevils are becoming extremely troublesome in both container grown plants and those in the garden. They produce small C shaped white larvae which feed on the roots of the plants causing their ultimate collapse. Not until the plants are beyond saving is the gardener aware that anything is amiss unless he knows what adult damage looks like. If there are small pieces removed from the edge of the leaves, then there is potential trouble brewing and an inspection of the soil around the plants should be made for grubs.

Dusting with a soil insecticidal dust or HCH dust exercises some control, particularly of the adult weevils. There are modern biological controls under investigation and these will shortly be available to the home gardener.

Diseases

The majority of fungal diseases outdoors can be controlled with a systemic fungicide. However, it is unwise to wait until the problem appears before spraying. With apple scab, for example, it is necessary to spray as the foliage just emerges during early spring and then to continue at three weekly intervals throughout the season.

Rusts are rather different. While a systemic fungicide will help to control troublesome rusts like leek rust, it is garden hygiene and the removal of carry-over debris that is most effective in providing a control. Once a rust disease has broken out contact copper fungicides help prevent spreading.

Some diseases, like potato scab, are caused by an actinomycete. There is no relliable cure. Grow resistant varieties and do not lime the soil.

Down-to-earth tip

Mice are a nuisance especially amongst newly sown seeds like peas and beans. To prevent them from stealing such seeds, mix a little paraffin with some dry sand and place it in a paper bag with the seeds. Shake vigorously so that the seeds become tainted. Sort them out from the sand and sow. The mice will leave them alone. The resulting plants will not be affected by the paraffin.

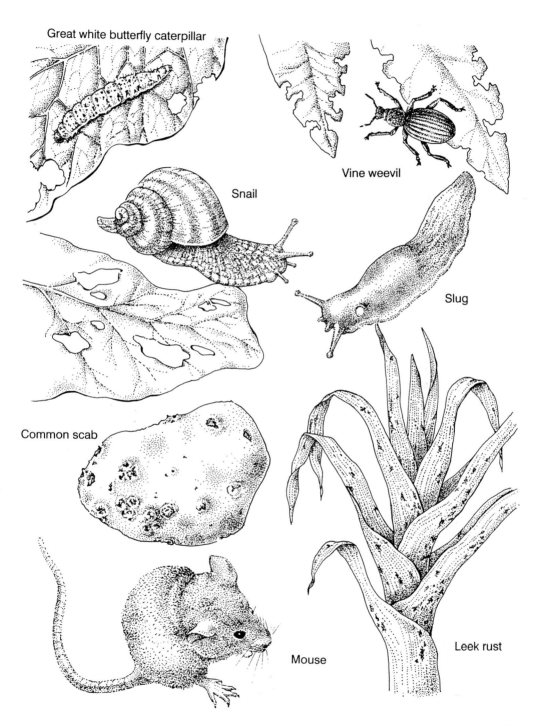

Great white butterfly caterpillar

Vine weevil

Snail

Slug

Common scab

Mouse

Leek rust

Pests and diseases under glass

There are many pests and diseases that can afflict plants that are grown indoors or in a greenhouse. While most can be controlled by pesticides of various kinds, much can be done by good hygiene. Do not allow dead leaves or faded flowers to remain clinging to plants or pots and always use sterilised compost and washed pots. When watering keep an eye open for tell-tale signs of trouble – spotted or chewed foliage, wilting stems or changes in foliage colour.

Pests

The opportunities for pests in a warm damp greenhouse are legion, but there is one that does not relish these conditions at all. This is the red spider mite, a widespread pest that only flourishes in warm dry conditions. It is common on carnations, foliage plants and indoor fruit, causing light mottling of the leaves and building a fine web beneath. While there are specific insecticides to cope with this pest, it can be kept at bay by regularly syringing the foliage.

Leaf hoppers cause the disfiguration of leaves and flowers of many indoor and outdoor plants. A contact insecticide based upon natural derivatives like pyrethrum and derris will control them. So will a systemic insecticide to a limited degree.

Some pests look rather like diseases and are very deceptive. Brown scale is one such creature which looks scarcely more than a brown scab. This innocuous looking creature is very damaging, clinging to foliage and sucking the sap. A systemic insecticide is absorbed by the sap stream and taken into the plant. When insects like scale and aphids puncture the plant tissue they take in the chemical and die. with a regular spraying regime the plants can be virtually innoculated against attack.

Diseases

Systemic fungicides work in a similar way to systemic insecticides and if sprayed early in the season can protect many plants against fungal attack. Grey mould on cucumbers and other plants can be controlled this way, although it is always as well to check carefully before spraying for one or two plants do have a sensitivity to certain systemic fungicides.

Most of the blights, like chrysanthemum blight, are only partially assisted by systemic fungicides, the control of these is very much more linked to growing conditions which are too humid and still. Good air circulation is vital, but contact fungicides can be useful in the early development stages of the disease.

Damping off disease and blackleg are both stem rots that are best controlled by a copper fungicide such as Cheshunt compound, although systemic fungicides will have a marked effect upon seedlings suffering from damping off when the foliage has appeared. Systemic fungicides only work when there is foliage to absorb them.

Other disorders

There are other disorders which look like pest or disease damage and which result from other factors. It may be stress, nutrient deficiency or irregular watering. Blossom end rot is a common problem with tomatoes when the end part of the fruit turns brown and is spoiled. It looks like a fungal disease, although the condition is brought about by stress and irregular watering. Blossom end rot is common with tomatoes which are growing in growing bags, when the top surface of the compost seems wet, but underneath it is dry.

Down-to-earth tip

Whitefly is a very difficult pest to get rid of, even modern insecticides having only partial success. Spraying has to be regular and varied with different active ingredients being used to ensure that they do not build up a resistance.

Spraying in the house is difficult anyway. However, colonies on individual plants can be despatched by using lard and a saucepan. Grease the inside of the saucepan, hold it over an infested plant and tap the pot. The flies will rise in the air and stick to the lard.

Do this regularly over a period of two weeks and the life cycle of the whitefly will be broken.

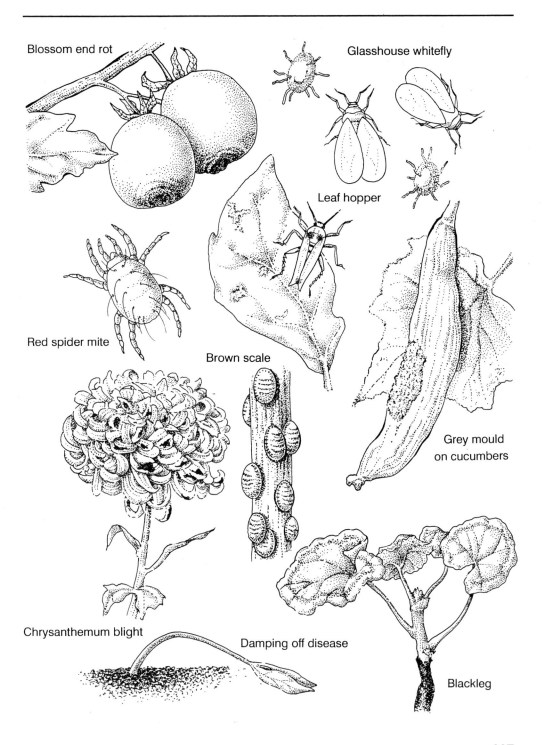

Blossom end rot

Glasshouse whitefly

Leaf hopper

Red spider mite

Brown scale

Grey mould
on cucumbers

Chrysanthemum blight

Damping off disease

Blackleg

GARDEN CENTRES

Strikes

Suppliers of the Best in Gardening for over 100 years

At Strikes Garden Centres you will find an exciting array of plants, shrubs and gardening equipment. In fact, you'll find outstanding displays and unrivalled choice — but more than that, you'll enjoy the experience of a thoroughly absorbing day out. To interest the non-gardener in the family there is giftware, books and even quality jams.

PLANTED IN 1877 AND STILL GROWING.

A family business …

The slogan reads "Planted in 1877 and still growing!" True! and always under the guidance of the Strike family whose attention to detail has seen the establishment of garden centres throughout Yorkshire, Cleveland and South Durham.

DISCOVER THE PLEASURE OF PLANTS

At your leisure ...

Browse through shrubs, trees and a myriad of plants all growing with your ultimate enjoyment in mind. And, even if the weather turns a little uncertain, then enjoy the displays in the large covered areas.

Choice and value ...

For the beginner or expert, Strikes provides outstanding value ... and even a guarantee! There are always experienced and trained staff on hand to give free expert advice, but above all else there's no pressure on your time – you can simply relax and enjoy the environment and – as many people do – return to enjoy another day.

DISCOVER THE PLEASURE OF PLANTS

FOR THE GREEN FINGERED AMONGST YOU... LOOK FOR THE BLUE SIGN!

COME TO STRIKES GARDEN CENTRES AND NURSERIES

... and enjoy an hour or two wandering round the delights a modern garden centre can offer. The choice is vast and offers everything and more to cater for both expert and amateur gardener. ... and remember all our container grown plants are guaranteed for a year.

Garden Centres and Nurseries at:-
MEADOWFIELDS, STOKESLEY • YORK ROAD, KNARESBOROUGH
COCKERTON, DARLINGTON • BOROUGHBRIDGE ROAD, NORTHALLERTON
SELBY ROAD, LEEDS 15 • REDHALL LANE, LEEDS 17

DISCOVER THE PLEASURE OF PLANTS

GARDEN CENTRES

Strikes

Suppliers of the Best in
Gardening for over 100 years

STRIKES
·Planted
in 1877 and
still growing!

DISCOVER THE PLEASURE OF PLANTS

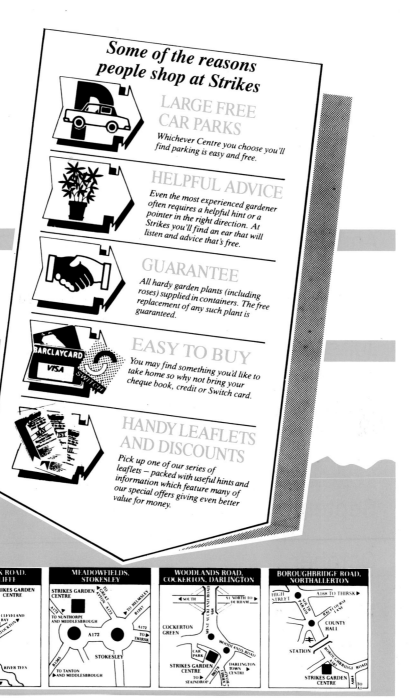

Some of the reasons people shop at Strikes

LARGE FREE CAR PARKS
Whichever Centre you choose you'll find parking is easy and free.

HELPFUL ADVICE
Even the most experienced gardener often requires a helpful hint or a pointer in the right direction. At Strikes you'll find an ear that will listen and advice that's free.

GUARANTEE
All hardy garden plants (including roses) supplied in containers. The free replacement of any such plant is guaranteed.

EASY TO BUY
You may find something you'd like to take home so why not bring your cheque book, credit or Switch card.

HANDY LEAFLETS AND DISCOUNTS
Pick up one of our series of leaflets – packed with useful hints and information which feature many of our special offers giving even better value for money.

ALSO AT

YORK ROAD, KNARESBOROUGH ● SELBY ROAD, LEEDS 15 ● REDHALL LANE, LEEDS 17

DISCOVER THE PLEASURE OF PLANTS

JOBS TO REMEMBER

January _____

February _____

March _____

April _____

May _____

June _____

July _____

August _____

September _____

October _____

November _____

December _____

BLACK&DECKER

GRASS TRIMMER

GL565C – 10"
TRIM'N'EDGE™ TRIMMER

2 tools in 1 – the versatility of a traditional grass trimmer plus an easy to use lawn edger. By simply pressing a button the head moves through 180° to transform the strimmer into an effective lawn edger.

2 tools in 1
Saves time and effort around the garden.

Secondary handle
Greater control and manoeuvrability especially whilst lawn edging.

Autofeed
Reduces the time and effort required by the user whilst trimming.

350 watt motor
Powerful motor allows cutting in tough grass & undergrowth.

CAT. NO.	GL565C
CUTTING SWATHE	10" (25cm)
LINE FEED SYSTEM	AUTOFEED
MOTOR POWER (watts)	350
CUTTING LINE (m)	9.0
EDGING FACILITY	YES
SECONDARY HANDLE	YES
CABLE LENGTH	12m (40ft)

BLACK&DECKER ®

GT243 – 24" BLADE BRAKE

Dual action blades
Reciprocating action improves cutting performance and reduces vibration.

Front guard
Protects the user's hand from the hedge.

Designed to tackle the toughest of hedges. A 24" blade will comfortably tackle hedges up to 100m in length. Dual action blades improve cutting performance and reduce vibration. Fitted with a number of safety features to protect the user.

Full bale handle
Improved control and manoeuvrability.

Precision ground blades
A film of oil is trapped between the blades improving performance and the life of the blades.

Safety blades
Blade openings narrow enough to stop fingers from getting cut.

AUTO STOP

Blade brake
Prevents accidents by stopping the blade within 2 seconds of the trigger being released.

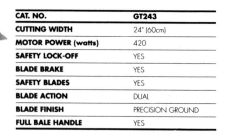

CAT. NO.	GT243
CUTTING WIDTH	24" (60cm)
MOTOR POWER (watts)	420
SAFETY LOCK-OFF	YES
BLADE BRAKE	YES
SAFETY BLADES	YES
BLADE ACTION	DUAL
BLADE FINISH	PRECISION GROUND
FULL BALE HANDLE	YES

ROTARY MOWER

GR450C – 16.5"
HIGH PERFORMANCE

Rear roller
Creates a traditional striped lawn finish.

Wheels flush with mower body
Allows cutting right up to the edge of the lawn.

Upswept handle
More comfortable to use and easier to push.

7 height of cut positions
Able to cope with almost any grass condition.

This new high performance mower offers all the features required by the gardener who takes pride in his work. The 16.5" cutting width makes light work of the larger lawn and the rear roller provides a traditional striped lawn finish.

CAT. NO.	GR450C
CUTTING WIDTH	16.5" (42cm)
MOTOR POWER (watts)	1500
SAFETY LOCK-OFF	YES
BLADE TYPE	METAL
BLADE BRAKE	YES
NO. OF CUTTING HEIGHTS	7
HANDLE TYPE	UPSWEPT
GRASS COLLECTION	FABRIC BAG
CABLE LENGTH	25m (82ft)

Blade brake
Reduces the risk of accidents by stopping the blade within 3 seconds.

Induction motor
Low maintenance/low noise motor which extends the life of the motor.

118

If you can read this much about compost, you probably need a Black & Decker shredder.

What's this rubbish? We refer to the pile of prunings and grass clippings in the corner of the garden that you call the compost heap. It's very kind of you to provide a home for woodlice and wasps but it isn't a lot of good as compost, is it? ¶ If you want to turn it into something you can use, you need to balance the nitrogen in the lawn clippings and soft green garden rubbish by adding kitchen waste and carbon rich wood. But to make that hard stuff appetising to the bacteria necessary for rotting you have to chop it into small pieces. ¶ No prizes for guessing the simplest way to increase the surface area of the contents of your heap by eight to ten times. You put it through the funnel of a Black & Decker shredder. (Branches go in the side chute). No sooner than it meets the hardened steel cutters than it will be reduced to the perfect texture for compost or mulch. Should you need to clear the cutters, you may notice how removing the cover of the shredder also cuts off the power and precludes any possibility of accidental operation. ¶ You may also notice a lack of chemical fertilisers, bonfires, trips to the dump and environment-unfriendly peat based composts. A very fair swop for unlimited supplies of dark brown, crumbly, sweet smelling, humus-rich compost. Even so, there are gardeners who might say a Black & Decker shredder is an unwarranted extravagance. To them we would say one thing: complete rot.

119

There is one cordless hedgetrimmer that will get you as far as the new Black & Decker.

The hand shears of course will get you as far, and further. As far, in fact, as your aching arms will take you. Despite their high consumption of elbow grease, we have to admit that hand shears have a lot going for them. You could even say we copied some of their best features in producing our new hedgetrimmer. Blades properly ground from thick steel, for a clean cutting edge. The lack of a lead (not to mention the lack of being held back by it, or the possibility of cutting through it). The equal weight distribution that makes our hedgetrimmer greet the hands like a favourite old tool. The bale handle, though, is something you won't find on hand shears. You can shift your grip around it, avoid getting locked into one position, as well as reach awkward corners. The red part under the bale handle, by the way, is the secondary safety switch. Take your hand off that or the handle switch and the blade brake instantly stops the cutting action. (Which actually is quite like the hand shears.) The power for our hedgetrimmer comes from the detachable Univolt power pack. It will power you for thirty minutes, enough to cut three hundred square feet of hedge. With the charger supplied you can recharge it in two hours or if you buy our Univolt fast charger, fifteen minutes. About as long, can we suggest, as it takes to recharge your own batteries when you've done that much cutting with your hand shears.

For a perfect lawn you need to go over it 18 times a year with 3 different tools.
Or do you need a Black & Decker Lawnraker?

Up. Down. Up. Down. Up. Down. Not the Grand Old Duke of York, but a gardener in full pursuit of the perfect lawn. Spring arrives to find him, his trusty tine rake in hand, sweeping up winter's traces, worm casts and having the year's first crack at the thatch. Thatch? It's that mat of fibrous material on top of the soil. If

1. SWEEPING. it gets too thick it blocks air and water circulation. But back to the gardener. The summer mowing season is hardly into its bi-weekly thrash when he's taken up his rake, dedicated once again, that this year will witness the final destruction of those mossy patches. Come autumn our

2. RAKING. gardener's a blur of activity. Barely has he finished scarifying (damned thatch again) with his rake, than he has to try and banish the drifts of falling leaves with his besom (that's what gardening books call a witches' broom).

Is it all worth it? Sure, by now the lawn's not looking too bad. But although our gardener's spent most of the summer on his lawn, he'll be very lucky if he's had the time to sit down on it. Unlike the gardener whose lawn is shown on the left. As you can see, he has equipped himself with a Black & Decker Lawnraker. It doesn't eliminate the going up and down. But if you've got a Black & Decker, you don't have to get black and blue. Put the tined roller 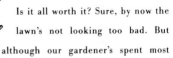 on the high setting

3. SCARIFYING. for sweeping; medium for light raking; and low for scarifying. There isn't a lot more to it. The Lawnraker comes complete with a collection box for all that lovely organic stuff you'll rake up. There's also a compactor to squash it down in the box, and halve your trips to the compost heap. We wouldn't like you going up and down the garden any more than you really have to.

◢◢ BLACK&DECKER®

SERIOUS TOOLS FOR SERIOUS GARDENERS.

BLACK & DECKER SERVICE CENTRES

ABERDEEN, 429 Union Street, Aberdeen, AB1 20A Tel: 0224 211442.

BELFAST, 232 Antrim Road, Glengormley, Newtownabbey, Co. Antrim, BT36 7QX. Tel: 0232 841071/2.

BIRMINGHAM, Long Acre, Birmingham, B7 5SL. Tel: 021-327 3411.

BLACKPOOL, 4 St. Annes Road, Blackpool, Lancs, FY4 2AA. Tel: 0253 408800.

BRADFORD, 5 John Street, Bradford, BD1 3JT. Tel: 0274 729332.

BRIGHTON, 89/90 London Road, Brighton, East Sussex, BN1 4JF. Tel: 0273 609391.

BRISTOL, 25/27 Stokes Croft, Bristol, BS1 3QA. Tel: 0272 245018.

CARDIFF 135 Maindy Road, Gabalfa, Cardiff, CF2 4HM. Tel: 0222 221547

CATFORD, 75 Rushey Green, Catford, SE6 4AF Tel: 081-698 9933

CHATHAM, 16A High View Drive, Maidstone Road, Chatham, Kent, ME5 9UN. Tel: 0634 684171.

COVENTRY, 23 Trinity Street, Coventry, CV1 IFJ. Tel: 0203 228691.

CROYDON, 89 London Road, Croydon, Surrey, CRO 2RF. Tel: 081-681 8049.

EDINBURGH, 33b Haddington Place, Leith Walk, Edinburgh, EH7 4AG. Tel: 031-556 8191.

GLASGOW, 272/280 Great Western Road, St George's Cross, Glasgow, G4 9EJ. Tel: 041-332 8000.

HUDDERSFIELD, 55 Lockwood Road, Huddersfield, HD1 3QU Tel: 0484 420492

HULL, 140 George Street, I, Hull, HU1 3AA. Tel: 0482 223587

LEEDS, 305 Dewsbury Road, Leeds, LS11 5LJ. Tel: 0532 714019.

LEICESTER, 41 Abbey Street, Leicester, LE1 3TE. Tel: 0533 627087.

LIVERPOOL, 49/51 London Road, Liverpool, L3 8HY. Tel: 051-207 1400.

LONDON-NORTH, 623 Holloway Road, London, N19 5SS. Tel: 071-272 8246.

LONDON-EAST, 746/748 Eastern Avenue, Green Gate, Newbury Park, Ilford, Essex, IG2 7HU. Tel: 081-518 6778.

LONDON-NORTHWEST, 9 Broadway Parade, Pinner Road, North Harrow, Middx, HA2 7SY. Tel: 081-863 6945.

LONDON-SOUTHWEST, 20 The Broadway, Tolworth, Surrey, KT 7HL. Tel: 081-399 6411.

LONDON-WEST, 15 Shield Drive, Westcross Centre, Brentford, Middlesex, TW8 9EX. Tel: 081-560 0885.

MANCHESTER, Commercial Street, Deansgate, Manchester, M15 4QB. Tel: 061-834 8865.

MIDDLESBROUGH, Bedford House, 112 Linthorpe Road, Middlesbrough, Cleveland, TSI 2JS. Tel: 0642 226826.

NEWCASTLE-upon-TYNE, 179-183 Shields Road, Byker, Newcastle, NE6 1DP. Tel: 091-2764422.

NORTHAMPTON, 75 Abington Street, Northampton, Northants, NN1 2BH. Tel: 0604 24697.

NORWICH, 28 Prince of Wales Road, Norwich, NR11LG. Tel: 0603 627600.

NOTTINGHAM, 361 Carlton Hill, Nottingham, NG4 1HX. Tel: 0602 873012.

PLYMOUTH, 65/67 Exeter Street, Plymouth, P14 0AH. Tel: 0752 227064

PORTSMOUTH, 122-124 London Road, Northend, Portsmouth, P02 9DE. Tel: 0705 667676.

READING, 28-34 Station Hill, Reading, Berks, RG1 1NF. Tel: 0734 504555.

SHEFFIELD, Unit 2, St Mary's House, 3 London Road, Sheffield, South Yorkshire, S2 4LA. Tel: 0742 760743

SLOUGH, 295 High Street, Slough, Berkshire, SL1 1BR. Tel; 0753 820445.

SOUTHAMPTON, Unit 2, Trinity Industrial Estate, Millbrook Road, Southampton, SOI 01A. Tel: 0703 780844.

SPENNYMOOR, Green Lane, Spennymoor, Co. Durham, DL16 6JG. Tel: 0388 422429

STOKE-ON-TRENT, Unit 2, York Street, Hanley, Stoke-on-Trent, Staffs, ST1 5ER. Tel: 0782 273455.

SWANSEA, 7 High Street, Swansea, SA1 1LE. Tel: 0792 467237.

SWINDON, 75 Cricklade Road, Gorse Hill South, Swindon, 5N2 1AA Tel: 0793 480840

WOLVERHAMPTON, Raglan Street, Chapel Ash, Wolverhampton, WV3 0ST. Tel: 0902 28181.

EIRE - DUBLIN, 14/15 Parliament Street, Dublin 2 Tel: 010 3531 777194.

ISLE OF MAN Repair Agent: Toolbox, Church Road, Port Erin, Isle of Man Tel: 0624 834901

CHANNEL ISLANDS For details of Service in the Channel Islands Contact:
Southampton Service Centre, Tel: 0703 780844.

MAIN OFFICE: Black & Decker Limited, Westpoint, The Grove, Slough, Berkshire SL1 1QQ
Telephone: Slough (0753) 511234, Fax: (0753) 551155.

Black & Decker reserve the right to alter without notice any product or product specification

Index

Cover Picture:

The garden at 30 Latchmere Road, Leeds, home of Mr and Mrs Joe Brown who open their gardens to the public every year to raise funds for the National Gardens Scheme charitable trust.

Published by The Northern Echo, Priestgate, Darlington, Co. Durham, DL1 1NF

© **The Northern Echo** / Philip Swindells